Reading the Qur'an in English

AN INTRODUCTORY GUIDE

Reading the Qur'an in English

AN INTRODUCTORY GUIDE

ROBERT A. CAMPBELL

Cape Breton University Press
Sydney, Nova Scotia, Canada

Cape Breton University Press recognizes the support of the Canada Council for the Arts, Block Grant program, and the Province of Nova Scotia, through the Department of Tourism, Culture and Heritage, for our publishing program. We are pleased to work in partnership with these bodies to develop and promote our cultural resources.

NOVA SCOTIA
Tourism, Culture and Heritage

Canada Council   Conseil des Arts
for the Arts   du Canada

Layout and Cover: Barry Gabriel, South Bar, NS
Printed in Canada on 100% recycled postconsumer fibre, certified EcoLogo and processed chlorine free, manufactured using biogas energy.

Library and Archives Canada Cataloguing in Publication

Campbell, Robert A., 1952-
    Reading the Qur'an in English: an introductory guide/Robert A. Campbell.

Includes bibliographical references.
ISBN 978-1-897009-40-6

    1. Koran--Criticism, interpretation, etc. 2. Koran--Hermeneutics.
3. Koran--Reading. 4. Islam. I. Title.
BP130.4.C34 2009   297.1'2261   C2009-900523-9

Cape Breton University Press
P.O. Box 5300
Sydney, Nova Scotia B1P 6L2 CA
www.cbu.ca/press

CONTENTS

Acknowledgements

This book is based on a series of lectures that I gave while teaching an introductory course on the Qur'an (HUMC17), in the fall terms of 2006 and 2007 at the Scarborough campus of the University of Toronto. In total, nearly 200 students, the majority of whom were Muslims, allowed me to take them on a journey through one of the world's most cherished, controversial and influential texts. This book is dedicated to them.

Thanks to Anne Fisher for her careful reading of the entire manuscript, and thanks to Barry Gabriel for the cover design and the layout of the book.

Robert Campbell
Sydney, Nova Scotia
January 2009

1

Approaching the Text
(Qur'an 108)

This book is intended to serve as a guide for those who are attempting to read the Qur'an in an English translation. I use the word "attempting" here because all too often people pick up one of the readily available translations of the Qur'an at their local library or bookstore with the best of intentions, only to be thrown off when they try to read it, by its unfamiliar structural and stylistic characteristics. Familiarity with the scripture of the Jews or Christians, or with standard literary forms such as the novel, builds a set of expectations about the use of narrative, description and dialogue to construct a story that appears to be breached by the Qur'an. Even though the potential reader might find much of the content to be familiar, the actual experience of reading the Qur'an often proves to be too jarring for many people. Consequently, they put the book down and remain frustrated about their attempts to read the text and to learn about Islam through the text.

It is unquestionably the case that the best way to learn about Islam is through reading the Qur'an, but this poses a major problem, not only for non-Muslims, but also for the vast majority of Muslims around the world. In several places (e.g., 12:2, 39:28, 43:3, 44:58) the Qur'an reminds us that it was revealed in Arabic so that Muhammad and his immediate audience could understand it. However, the Qur'an is written in Classical Arabic, an old form of the language that not many speakers of modern Arabic dialects understand well enough to allow them to read and comprehend the scripture. At the same time, it is important to realize that Arabic is not the first language of the vast majority of the world's Muslims. Indonesia and Pakistan have Muslim populations much larger than all of the Arab nations combined, and furthermore, not all Arabs are Muslims.

Traditionally, as young children, Muslims learn to read the Arabic text of the Qur'an in part, so that they can recite portions of it during daily prayer. In this instance reading implies solely sounding out the text. Their knowledge of the content of the Qur'an tends to come from secondary sources written in their native languages. Nowadays, wherever there are large concentrations of Muslims, recitations of the Qur'an can be heard in the mosques and schools, and even in the streets. Beyond that, there are radio stations and

Robert A. Campbell

websites that broadcast qur'anic recitations 24/7, all around the globe. However, this does not mean that knowledge of the text is equally pervasive. Many young Muslims attempt to memorize large portions of the Qur'an, and their families and their communities hold those who learn the entire text by heart in high esteem. Yet, even those who have accomplished this impressive feat are unlikely to understand, to any great extent, what they are reciting. Thus, it is clear that the potential readership for translations of the Qur'an extends well beyond curious non-Muslims.

According to Islam, one of the most significant characteristics of the Qur'an as a divine revelation is that it was revealed in Arabic. The Arabic language is viewed as perfect and unsurpassed in purity of form and meaning, and thus it is viewed as the ideal and only appropriate medium for the transmission of what Muslims consider to be the last and final revelation of God's will to humanity (Omar 2003: 15D-17D). The question of whether the Qur'an was in fact a divine revelation is not our concern here. The fact that Muslims believe this to be the case is enough, and in many ways, this belief is one of the main reasons we might be interested in reading the Qur'an in the first place. However, because of the inseparability of the Qur'an from the Arabic language, any translation of the Qur'an is viewed as a human interpretation of the text, not to be confused with the sacred text itself. Having said that, it is unlikely that most Muslims today, not to mention the vast majority of non-Muslims, will take the opportunity to undergo the difficult and prolonged study of Classical

3

Arabic that would allow them to read and understand the Qur'an as it was revealed. As a result, it is important to determine if there is any merit at all in reading the Qur'an in translation.

Simply put, the answer is yes, but it is imperative to point out that one of the core assumptions of the present work is that reading the Qur'an in translation does not replace reading the Qur'an in Arabic. Rather, it is complementary to it. For one thing, there is an aesthetic aspect associated with reading and listening to the Qur'an in Arabic that is clearly impossible to reproduce no matter how skilled the translator (Nelson 2001; Sells 1999). On this point, I completely agree. Similarly, if we accept that the Arabic language is the perfect medium for the Qur'an, then it is likely that there are some theological and spiritual facets of the text that are dependent on this linguistic relationship. Regarding this point I would suggest that contemporary readers, even those well schooled in Classical Arabic, are not living in early seventh century Arabia and thus, they are just as removed from the original historical and linguistic context within which the Qur'an came into being as anyone else. These issues notwithstanding, much of the historical, legal, sociological and religious content of the Qur'an is accessible to us through reading a translation.

How is Islam related to Judaism and Christianity? Do these three religions share the same God? What prophets and personalities from history and other religious traditions are mentioned in the Qur'an, and what does it say about them? How is Islam to be practised?

How should Muslims relate to non-Muslims? Does the Qur'an advocate war? Does the Qur'an advocate the oppression of women? What does it say about this life and the next life? These are a few examples of the sorts of questions that we can hope to find answers to by reading a translation of the Qur'an, that is, by treating it as a source book through which we can increase our knowledge of a major religious tradition, one that is growing rapidly and is second only to Christianity in numbers of adherents around the globe. This, to my mind, is the greatest justification for attempting to translate sacred texts into modern languages and for learning to read these translations in such a way that we can increase our understanding of Islam.

My Approach

In my view, introductory books on the Qur'an are often hampered by one or more of the following characteristics. First, some books assume too much prior familiarity with the structure and content of the Qur'an, whether in Arabic or in translation. In other words, they appear to be written to those who, having read the Qur'an, are now trying to understand what they have read. Second, as implied by much of the preceding discussion, many books assume a fairly sophisticated understanding of linguistic theory and methodology, and more particularly Arabic language and linguistics. This limits the potential readership for such books to a small number of specialists and makes the books inappropriate even for many advanced undergraduate students of religion, let alone the general public. Third, these books tend to focus on controversies around such issues as authorship, textual variants, circumstances of revelation, and abrogation, from both a scholarly and a sectarian perspective. Again, these matters only make sense once a high degree of familiarity with the Qur'an, the history of its analysis and textual criticism more generally, has been acquired. Very few introductory books respond to the basic questions of what is in the Qur'an and what might a contemporary reader find of interest or significance in the sacred text of Islam. Thus, there is still a need for truly introductory books on the Qur'an, especially ones that recognize that the majority of people interested in reading the Qur'an are going to be reading it in translation, with the intention of discovering just what it is that the Qur'an contains.

In an effort to meet this need, the present work is informed by the recent trend in qur'anic scholarship that Abdullah Saeed (2006) refers to as "contextualist." This approach to understanding and interpreting the Qur'an does not confine itself to purely linguistic criteria, nor does it support the notion that the experience and insights of the first centuries of Islam can somehow be transported forward to meet the needs of modern day readers. Rather, it is based on the idea that a broader understanding of the changing sociohistorical context of the Qur'an, and of Islam more generally, needs to be taken into account when trying both to comprehend and apply the scripture to present circumstances.

In this book, I try to provide a way for readers to begin reading the Qur'an in translation that will en-

courage them to read further. I accomplish this in part
through the order in which I suggest that passages from
the Qur'an be read, and in part, by the various methods that I introduce as tools to help the reader analyze
and understand what they are reading. It is important
to remember, while reading this book and while reading the Qur'an, that I am making suggestions – I am
not trying to argue for one particular way of understanding the Qur'an. At the same time, no one approaches a text as a blank slate. The lessons that people
learn from reading the Qur'an will depend on what
they bring with them to their study of the Qur'an, in
terms of their religious upbringing, their educational
background, and their basic motivation (historical, religious, socio-political) for wanting to read the Qur'an
in the first place.

Unless otherwise specified, all excerpts from the
Qur'an are taken from the English translation of Muhammad Abdel Haleem (2005). From this point forward, when I refer to the Qur'an, I mean the English
translation of the Qur'an. I do not provide excerpts
from the Qur'an or other sources in Arabic script, or as
transliterations of Arabic words into Latin letters. Similarly, with the exception of a few words like *barzakh,
basmalah* and *hadith*, for which I offer an explanation
when they are introduced, I have avoided using Arabic
terms to designate key concepts. I do however use the
word surah as a designation for what are generally referred to as the individual chapters of the Qur'an. In a
literal sense the word surah means wall, enclosure or
step, and is related to a verb form meaning to climb

or elevate (Omar 2003: 277). As much as possible, in terms of sources throughout the text, I have tried to refer to books and articles by contemporary authors that are readily available in English. References to better-known ancient authors are generally made through secondary sources.

Over all, I choose to be a pragmatic realist with respect to certain elements of Islam. With well over a billion adherents around the world, it does me little good to question the fundamental beliefs and practices of Islam. From my perspective, there is little value in spending time arguing about whether Muhammad ever existed, or whether he was the author of the Qur'an. Scholars with different agendas have produced several volumes in which they entertain these issues. I am much more interested in looking at the contemporary situation through a sociological lens. In other words, I am concerned with the consequences that the belief in the divine nature of the Qur'an and its revelation to Muhammad, have for Muslims and non-Muslims in today's world. Thus, the basic premise of this book is quite simple: the more that people can learn about Islam through the Qur'an, and the more people that do learn about Islam through the Qur'an, the better.

I do however, operate under one assumption that some might find controversial. Following Gerald Hawting (1999), I take seriously the suggestion that as a religion, Islam emerged primarily within the context of competing monotheisms, Judaism and Christianity, rather than solely out of an environment of literal pagan idolatry and polytheism. Consequently, even though my focus is on the text

8

of the Qur'an, from time to time, I refer to the scripture of the Jews and Christians as well as to aspects of the so-called 'period of ignorance' that preceded the establishment of Islam in Arabia (Sicker 2000).

The Structure of the Qur'an

The Qur'an is divided into 114 sections called surahs, which are often referred to in English as chapters. The word chapter however, is quite misleading because it tends to imply a thematic unity and narrative structure that is uncharacteristic of the Qur'an. Rather, the surahs should be looked at as bundles or containers of discrete passages, varying in length and theme. The surahs range in length from surah 2, with 286 verses, to surah 108, with three verses. Beginning with the second surah, the surahs are arranged roughly in decreasing order of length. As Neal Robinson (2003: 259) points out, there is a precedent for this type of ordering in the New Testament with respect to the epistles of Paul, which are arranged from the longest (Romans) to the shortest (Philemon), with only a couple of easily explained exceptions. The first surah, known as *The Opening*, is only seven verses long, and it plays a special role in the Qur'an and in the practice of Islam (see chapter 3). The verses are also of varying length, with the shortest verse (55:1) consisting of only one Arabic word, and the longest (2:282) containing about 240 English words in translation.

The shorter, chronologically earlier surahs, which are also for the most part constructed with shorter verses, tend to be based on a single theme. Longer later surahs combine several themes or episodes and often, but not always, exhibit the following structural characteristics:

> prologue (introductory, or linking passage)
> several narrative segments (based on a single theme)
> interpolations (diversions, or shifts away from a
> theme)
> epilogue (concluding, or linking passage)

Not all of these elements are always present in a surah, and the length of each component, particularly of the narrative segments, can vary greatly. I provide this pattern primarily as an analytical tool to help readers break down the surahs into more understandable units. However, readers must be cautious not to force this pattern onto any particular surah. At the same time, using this tool helps to demonstrate the sophisticated and coherent overall structure of the Qur'an that might not be initially evident as the reader moves through the text.

Often, the narrative segments can appear to constitute coherent stories on their own, as if they were independent smaller surahs. Similarly, a sequence of narrative segments will sometimes appear to relate a similar message, with perhaps a different individual or historical event being used in each case. For example, in several surahs (e.g., 26, 51), the stories of Noah, Abraham, Moses, Hud, Salih and other prophets are related, one after the other, to make the single point that people have continually failed to heed the warning that has been sent to them by God through His chosen messengers.

The prologues and epilogues provide a broader context for the surahs and often serve to link them with the Qur'an in general or with the mission of the Prophet. For example, the second verse of surah 2 states that the Qur'an contains guidance for the faithful, thus linking the surah to the request for guidance presented in the first surah. One of the best-known prologues is the discussion of the night journey that appears in the opening verses of surah 17, which I discuss in greater detail in chapter 10. One of the functions of an epilogue, for example at the end of surah 11 (verse 120), is to explain to the Prophet that the stories of former prophets are being related to him as a means of strengthening his faith and his dedication to the mission for which he has been chosen. Thus this verse acts as a link between the story of Hud (surah 11) and the story of Joseph (surah 12).

The interpolations break up longer lessons or narrative segments, and can sometimes appear to be completely unrelated to the surrounding verses. At the same time, it can also be argued that these inserts act as mechanisms for sharpening focus on particular points, or more generally, to refresh the attention of the reader. So for example, just before the end of a lengthy discussion on family matters in surah 2, verses 219 to 242, we find two verses (238-239) on prayer that are seemingly out of place, diverting our attention away from the main theme. Irfan Ahmad Khan (2005: 599) suggests that the purpose of these two verses is to remind believers that they cannot follow the commandments laid out

11

in the surrounding verses without attending to their obligations to pray.

Another common feature of the structure of the surahs is the way that contrasting passages are placed close together, so that the meaning and implications of the opposing themes are clear to the reader. These passages are often separated by verses that relate a lesson or condition pertinent to the contrasted elements. If we take surah 108, *Abundance*, the shortest surah in the Qur'an as an example, we read:

> *We have truly given abundance to you [Prophet] –*
> *pray to your Lord and make your sacrifice to Him alone –*
> *it is the one who hates you who has been cut off.* (108:1-3)

In these three short lines, opposing themes are separated by a command. In the first and third phrases, the abundance that the Prophet will reap is contrasted to the one who hates him who will be cut off. In the middle line however, as a conditional statement, the Prophet is reminded to pray and make sacrifices only to God, the source of these words. Thus, we are introduced to a major recurring theme throughout the Qur'an, that God rewards those who follow His commands and punishes those who do not.

As will be discussed in chapter 4, there is only one surah (12) that displays the sort of thematic and structural unity that would lead us to refer to it as a chapter in the conventional sense. Scholars are divided on whether there is any merit at all in treating complete surahs, especially the longer ones, holistically for purposes of analysis or interpretation. The tendency has been rather, to deal with individual verses or groups of verses, while for the most part ignoring their placement, or potential function, within the context of a particular surah. Even though passages in one part of the Qur'an are regularly used to explain passages in other locations (the Qur'an as its own commentary), less attention has been paid to using the various passages within a single surah as a basis for understanding other passages in the same surah. More recently, there has been a shift towards trying to understand the surahs as unified constructions, with a layer of meaning that goes beyond that of their component parts. So for example, Ashraf Ali Thanavi claims that the overall theme of surah 31 (*Luqman*) is the Qur'an and the way that the scripture presents the notion of the Oneness of God (Mir 2004b: 200). Illustrations of these alternate approaches to studying the text will be provided in later chapters.

The Names of the Surahs

Each of the surahs has a particular name, but these names should not be viewed as chapter titles. Rather, among other things, they can reflect the names of individuals mentioned within the surah, or particular incidents that are recounted therein. Thus, some, such as *Joseph* (12), *Abraham* (14), *Mary* (19), *Luqman* (31), *Sheba* (34), *Muhammad* (47), and *Noah* (71), are named after prophets or important historical figures. Others, such as *Thunder* (13), *The Bee* (16), *The Star* (53), *The*

Moon (54), *The Constellations* (85), *The Sun* (91), and *The Fig* (95) appear to refer to aspects of God's creation. Still others, such as *Repentance* (9), *Kneeling* (45), *The Hypocrites* (63), *The Resurrection* (75) and *Clear Evidence* (98) hint at more theological themes or aspects of religion. A small number, such as *Ya Sin* (36) and *Qaf* (50), take their names from the isolated Arabic letters that appear at the beginning of the surah (see chapter 9 for a discussion of these letters).

Farid Esack (2005: 61) points out that the names of the surahs have never been of much concern to Islamic scholars. According to one tradition, the names served an organizational purpose, allowing scribes to place newly revealed material in its correct location according to the instructions of Muhammad.

The Qur'an in English

The first English translation of the Qur'an was prepared in 1649 by Alexander Ross, a school teacher who knew no Arabic and who based his translation on an earlier French version by André du Ryer. George Sale's translation dates from 1734 and it remained popular for more than two hundred years, partially because of the helpful comments and notes in italics that he embedded in the text.

With respect to modern English translations, among those produced by non-Muslims, the one by Arthur J. Arberry in 1955 demonstrates a great respect for the rhythm and grammar of the Arabic language, and hence is popular with scholars. Better known perhaps is the translation of N. J. Dawood, an Iraqi Jew living in England, published by Penguin in 1956, which has since gone through four revisions. This translation has been criticized for taking too many liberties with the text, and for placing the surahs out of order. Among English speaking Muslims, the 1930 translation prepared by Muhammad Marmaduke Pickthall, an English Christian convert to Islam, shows respect for the Arabic language, but employs an outdated formal English style.

Abdullah Yusuf Ali, a Muslim born in India, produced a translation with commentary in 1937 that has the Arabic and English text in parallel columns and provides extensive notes on the lower half of each page. His version is quite detailed and extremely useful, but also employs outdated language. Another well-researched version with extensive notes is that of Muhammad Asad, a Polish Jew who converted to Islam, published in 1980. His version has been criticized by Islamic theologians for taking too many liberties with the language, but it is gaining in popularity. Comparing the translations of Yusuf Ali and Asad, Muzaffar Iqbal (2004: 294) indicates that while Yusuf Ali was more concerned with the inner meaning of the Qur'an as the divine word, a timeless ethical and moral code, Asad viewed the Qur'an as a message for modern Muslims, one that would inform an Islamic renaissance.

As mentioned in the introduction, excerpts from the Qur'an cited throughout this text are taken from the translation of Muhammad A. S. Abdel Haleem (2005), who was born in Egypt and now teaches Arabic at the University of London. He explains that his translation "is intended to go further than previous works in accuracy, clarity, flow, and currency of language... written in a modern easy style, avoiding where possible the use of cryptic language or archaisms that tend to obscure meaning" (xxix). In order to demonstrate just how varied the translations can be, the following are excerpts from selected translations of the first six verses of surah 55:

> *The Merciful has taught his servant the Koran. He created man: he hath taught him distinct speech. The sun and the moon run their courses according to a certain rule: and the vegetables which creep on the ground and the trees submit to his disposition.* (Sale)

> *The All-merciful has taught the Koran. He created man and He taught him the explanation. The sun and the moon to a reckoning, and the stars and trees bow themselves.* (Arberry)

> *The Beneficent has made known the Qur'an. He has created man. He has taught him utterance. The sun and the moon are made punctual. The stars and the trees worship.* (Pickthall)

> *(Allah) Most Gracious! It is He Who has taught the Qur'an. He has created man: He has taught him speech (and intelligence). The sun and the moon follow courses (exactly) computed; And the herbs and the trees — both (alike) bow in adoration.* (Yusuf Ali)

16

It is the Lord of Mercy who taught the Qur'an. He created man and taught him to communicate. The sun and the moon follow their calculated courses; the plants and the trees submit to His designs; (Haleem)

With the exception of the Yusuf Ali version, these translators place the verses in paragraph form, as I have done here. Unlike what I have done here, each of these translators except Arberry and Pickthall number the individual verses.

Commentary on the Qur'an

One of the most interesting features of the Qur'an that distinguishes it from the scripture of Judaism and Christianity is that it provides a commentary on itself (Haleem 1999: 158-83). Accepting that the Qur'an was revealed over a period of about twenty years, it makes sense that some later portions would elaborate on earlier verses, and thus scholars look first to see if there are internal clues to help us understand a particular passage. Aids to interpreting the Qur'an can also be found in the *hadith* collections that record the sayings and life-example of Muhammad, as witnessed by his companions and passed on through generations until they were finally collected and written down a couple of hundred years after the Prophet's death (Cleary 2001). There is also a long tradition of systematic commentaries on the Qur'an, known as *tafsir*, that tend to provide a verse by verse analysis of the text. For the most part these follow what Saeed (2006) refers to as a "textualist" or "semi-textualist" approach, in which great attention is given to the grammar and syntax of Classical Arabic, and where precedence is given to what the text would have meant at the time it was revealed. More recently, scholars have been producing thematic commentaries, such as those by Fazlur Rahman (1994) and Abdel Haleem (1999), in which several different passages that display common elements or themes are handled together, irrespective of their location in the text. Still other modern commentators such as Mu-hammad al-Ghazali (2000) combine a verse-by-verse method with a thematic approach. Examples of these different sources and methods will be provided in the chapters that follow.

Reading Order

In order to get the most out of reading this book, it is advisable to read and re-read sections from the Qur'an as you go along. While I recommend the Haleem (2005) translation, you might want to try a few different trans-lations to find the one that you are most comfortable reading. Irrespective of which version you choose, the following surahs (numbers in brackets, with numbers following a colon indicating specific verses within a surah) should be read prior to reading the correspond-ing chapters (one through ten) in this book: one (108), two (96, 74, 73, 68, 111), three (1, 112, 114, 24: 35), four (12), five (26, 27, 28), six (31, 19:16-40, 18:83-102), seven (99, 81, 82, 101, 50), eight (55, 56), nine (2) and ten (17). Reference to these specific readings is repeated underneath the title of each chapter. Beyond this, I recommend that the Qur'an be read in reverse, starting with the smaller surahs and moving towards the longer more complex surahs as one becomes more comfortable with the style and content. In terms of understanding the text, there is no appreciable advantage, whether logical or theological, in trying to read the Qur'an from beginning to end.

2

Revelation
(Qur'an 96, 74, 73, 68, 111)

The Call

*Read! In the name of Your Lord who created: He created
man from a clinging form. Read! Your Lord is the Most
Bountiful One who taught by [means of] the pen, who
taught man what he did not know. (96:1-5)*

These few lines are considered by the majority of Muslims to constitute the first revelation made to Muhammad through the angel
Gabriel. The word "through" is important because the
Qur'an is believed to come from God, and thus, just as
Muhammad is regarded strictly as the recipient of the
revelation, Gabriel is merely the transmitter or con-
duit of the revelation, not its author. In this short passage, several themes are introduced that are essential

to understanding the Qur'an and Islam more broadly. Specifically, these verses clarify the nature of God, the relationship of God to humankind, and the way that God communicates with people.

The opening command to read in verse 1, or to "recite" as it is often translated, signals Muhammad's role as a messenger of God, and it also serves by extension as an instruction for all Muslims to recite the message received by Muhammad. According to tradition, Gabriel came to Muhammad while he was meditating in a cave outside Makkah and taking hold of him, instructed him to recite. Muhammad objected by saying that he could not read, but Gabriel squeezed him harder and repeated the command.

The initial instruction to read is followed by a conditional statement indicating that Muhammad is to read in the name of the Lord. Thus, the act of remembering or calling upon God is linked eternally with the act of reading, and serves to clarify to those who will hear the Qur'an that the authority of the message resides with God. As a result, the practice of invoking God becomes a standard feature of the Qur'an, with the phrase "In the name of God, The Lord of Mercy, the Giver of Mercy" being placed at the beginning of all the surahs, except surah 9 (chapter 3). By extension, this practice of invoking the name of God when carrying out an action is a constituent part of almost every aspect of Muslim daily life. Furthermore, this Lord that is referred to in the opening verses of surah 96 is not just any Lord; it is the Lord who created and more specifically, the Lord who created humankind.

We might wonder how to interpret the focus on
a creator Lord in the context of the origins of Islam.
Against a background of polytheism or paganism, this
identification signals that it is not some local deity, or
minor god, but rather it is the one who created everything that exists – including the message, the messenger, and all those who would hear the message.
By contrast, when viewed within the context of the
other Abrahamic faiths, Judaism and Christianity, calling upon the creator of all things in these verses links
Islam with the Genesis account of the creation of the
universe and the first humans. Interestingly, whereas
in Genesis (2:7), humans are created out of clay, the
account in this surah appears to some interpreters to
more closely resemble a modern scientific understanding of embryology (Bucaille 1979). The reference to a
clinging form might also reflect the more sociological-
ly significant point of the importance of bloodlines in
terms of establishing patterns of protection and inheritance among the tribal societies of Arabia. According
to some interpreters, the notion of the clinging form
can be interpreted as a symbol of the utter dependence
of humans on God (Haleem 2005: 428).

The repetition of the instruction to read can be interpreted simply as a means of emphasizing a point –
a common literary device in the Hebrew Bible (Alter
1981: 88-113). However, it also introduces a shift in
the focus of the message. In this instance the invocation
is made more specific through the indication of one
of the attributes of the Lord, namely, that this Lord is
bountiful, a term that can be interpreted to imply a

23

gracious giver of blessings. Here, the gift is teaching and the mechanism of that teaching is the pen. Teaching implies that there is something to be taught and that the recipient is capable of learning. Both of these ideas hint at the special place that humans have in God's creation. Yet, they also imply that there are things that humans cannot grasp on their own, thus reiterating the notion of dependence associated with the clinging form. As a consequence, the revelation of the Qur'an can be viewed as a necessary part of the completion of the relationship between God and humans. The mention of the pen is also very important because up to this point, the Arab culture had relied on oral transmission of its history and its literary heritage. The Qur'an becomes the first written work in Arabic, providing a standardized record to act as a scriptural foundation for Islam, while at the same time providing a concrete link between Islam and the previous religions of the book, namely, Judaism and Christianity.

Presenting the first five verses of surah 96 more schematically gives us the ability to analyze the text in a different way. Through this method, we are able to see the parallels between the two sections of the passage, and it reinforces the notion that with a good translation, many elements of the structure and content of the Qur'an are still accessible to those who cannot read Arabic. The two sections are labeled 1 and 2, and the number 3 is used to identify a pair of verses (the first of which is also part of section 2) that appear to constitute an overall conclusion emerging out of the two preparatory sections. I use the following terms (labelled with small letters) to identify the components of the sections: (a) instruction, (b) invocation, (c) action, (d) recipient, (e) mechanism, (f) condition and (g) benefit.

1a. Read!	*2a. Read!*
1b. In the name of the Lord	*2b. Your Lord is the Most Bountiful One*
1c. who created:	*2c. who taught*
	2e. (3f) [by means] of the pen,
1d. He created man	*2d. who taught man*
1e. from a clinging form.	
	3g. what he did not know.

As already mentioned, the instruction (a) is to Muhammad and to all who will read the message. The invocation (b) is in the name of the Lord and more specifically, to a giving Lord. The action (c) is first to create and then to teach. Humans are the recipients (d) of both of these actions, and the mechanisms (e) differ inasmuch as the first is biological (clinging form) and the second is mechanical (pen). There is a shift in the order of these elements and the addition of a new element occurring in the second section that requires explanation.

The break in the expected order of elements in the second section, in which 2e is placed ahead of 2d, can be viewed as a stylistic device to set up the expectation that something else is going to follow, namely, the final statement labelled 3g. In fact, the whole sequence would still make perfectly good sense if 2e followed 2d, but the shift moves the word "man" closer to the word "know," reinforcing the fact that humanity is reliant on God for knowledge. Thus, the statement "[by means] of the pen" serves in the first instance as a mechanism (2e), and in the second instance as a condition (3f). That is, the pen, or writing (scripture), is not only the means through which God teaches humanity, but it is the condition, or the only way that humans can gain true knowledge (the benefit). Thus, the final statement (3g), which constitutes a conclusion to the whole passage, appears to answer the question: "Why read?" It is an answer for Muhammad at the time of the first revelation and it is an answer for everyone who picks up the Qur'an from that point forward.

The record of this initial revelation in the Qur'an is followed by a sequence of additional verses that, in combination, constitute the surah known alternately as *The Clinging Form*, or *Read*. The remaining verses (6-19) focus on a single theme and can be divided into five sub-sections, each with its own emphasis. The overall subject of these verses is the condemnation of an opponent of Muhammad who has been trying to prevent the believers from practising their religion. Verses 6 through 8 contain a comment on the tendency of humans to overestimate their abilities, thinking themselves self-sufficient. This part of the message could be interpreted as a direct link to the previous verses, reiterating the theme of dependency. The next two sub-sections (9-12 and 13-14) express a strong admonition, first of those who try to prevent the believers from praying and second, of those who deny the truth of the message brought by the Prophet. The fourth sub-section (15-18) is a warning of what will happen to opponents of Islam, and the final sub-section (19) is a direction to Muhammad to bow down and draw near to God through prayer.

One question that arises from this analysis is whether these additional verses were revealed at the same time as the first five. If they were, then how can we account for the fact that verses 6 through 19 refer to events that clearly took place at a later period, when Islam was at least adequately established to produce opponents? If they were not, then does the final structural arrangement demonstrate that there is a deeper logic to the Qur'an as a whole?

If we accept the notion that surahs in the Qur'an were constructed out of one or more clusters of verses that may have been revealed at different times, then we might suggest that verses 6 through 19 were a later addition to the initial five verses. However, if we accept the idea that this surah reflects thematic and structural unity, then we might agree with some modern commentators such as Amin Aslan Islahi, that this surah was revealed in its entirety at one time, and therefore cannot have been the first to be revealed (Mir 2004b: 205). Whatever the case, it is interesting to note that an examination of the surah as a whole demonstrates a parallel to surah 108, examined in the previous chapter, where a conditional statement separates two contrasting passages. In surah 96 the contrasting passages, verses 1 to 5 (reward) and verses 6 to 18 (punishment), occur one after the other, with the conditional verse (19) coming at the end. Even though the order and length of each element is different in both cases, this overall three-part structure is a common literary construction throughout the Qur'an.

The Prophet of Islam

Although our focus is on the Qur'an rather than on Islam more generally, some insight into the life of the Prophet of Islam would be instructive at this point. Muhammad was born in Makkah in 570 CE. He was raised primarily by his grandfather and then his uncle Abu Talib. He became a successful merchant and, at about age 25, married his employer Khadija who was 15 years his senior. At age 40, while meditating in a cave outside Makkah during the month of Ramadan, he received the first revelation. These encounters with Gabriel would continue intermittently for 23 more (lunar) years.

According to Neal Robinson (2003: 38), initially, between the years 610-614, Muhammad shared his message in secret with close family and associates. Consistent with this notion, Islamic tradition suggests that some of the early surahs (e.g., 108, 111, 74 and 68) are directed at particular individuals, but they also establish the fundamentals of the faith (surahs 1 and 112). The next period (614-617) is marked by public preaching and growing opposition from the people of Makkah, as the Prophet called for the abandonment of the old gods and of outmoded tribal ways. In a third phase (617-622), opposition grew to the point where trade and marriage boycotts were established against

Muhammad's tribe, the Quraysh. For many years, the Prophet had been protected by his uncle but in 619, with the deaths of both Khadija and Abu Talib, the Prophet faced unprecedented challenges. During this phase, in 620, tradition relates that Muhammad took a night journey (see chapter 10), aided by the angel Gabriel, first to Jerusalem and then into heaven, where among other things he met with Moses. Two years later (622), at the invitation of the people of Yathrib (later called Madina), he migrated north to form the first Islamic community. The Islamic calendar begins from the time of this migration.

In 630, after almost a decade of hostile encounters between the Makkans and the growing Islamic community in Madina, the Prophet marched into Makkah with his army, but instead of engaging in battle, he offered a general amnesty leading many of his opponents to convert to Islam. The content of the surahs during this time reflect the needs of the expanding community and serve to demarcate Islam from the old religious traditions of Arabia, as well as from Judaism and Christianity. Muhammad continued to live in Madina, making his final pilgrimage to Makkah just before his death in 632. During this trip, he received what is considered by many Muslims to be the final revelation:

> - *the disbelievers have already lost hope that you will give up your religion. Do not fear them: fear Me. Today I have perfected your religion for you, completed My blessing upon you, and chosen as your religion Islam: total devotion to God;* (5:3)

As with the initial revelation, in this passage Muhammad is not referred to by name. As reading the Qur'an will demonstrate, even though the Prophet is constantly addressed throughout the text, he is only mentioned by name in four places (3:144, 33:40, 47:2 and 48:29). One possible interpretation of this phenomenon is that readers are to associate the Qur'an with God and not Muhammad.

There are many biographies of Muhammad, and there continues to be a lively tradition of writing the life story of the Prophet for the spiritual edification of the faithful (e.g., Mubarakpuri 2002). The earliest biography is attributed to Ibn Ishaq (d. 768), but we only have this text in various later edited and supplemented versions, the most famous of which is by Ibn Hisham (d. 828). Among more recent biographies, those by Maxime Rodinson (1980), Martin Lings (1983), and Karen Armstrong (1991) are informative and well researched. Particularly noteworthy for their presentation of alternate views on the life of the Prophet and the origins of Islam are the works of Crone and Cook (1977), and Nevo and Koren (2003).

Makkah and Madina

Consistent with the sequence of events in the life of the Prophet, it makes sense to assume that some of the surahs of the Qur'an were revealed in Makkah, while others were revealed after the journey to Madina. Consequently, several scholars have suggested an ordering of the surahs based on their content and on the perceived circumstances of revelation. Also, consistent with the decreasing length rule discussed in the previous chapter, the arrangement of the surahs in the Qur'an does not reflect the order in which they were revealed. In many Arabic and translated editions of the Qur'an, the reported order of revelation is based on the one published in the 1925 Cairo printing of the Qur'an (Robinson 2003: 72-74). There is no substantial evidence to suggest that this ordering is any more accurate, from the perspective of faith or scholarship, than any other; it is merely the most familiar. The following is the order of the surahs according to the so-called Nöldeke-Schwally classification system, based on extensive linguistic analysis carried out primarily by non-Muslim German researchers in the late nineteenth century (Robinson 2003: 77-78):

First Makkan: 96, 74, 111, 106, 108, 104,
107, 102, 105, 92, 90, 94, 93, 97, 86, 91,
80, 68, 87, 95, 103, 85, 73, 101, 99, 82, 81,
53, 84, 100, 79, 77, 78, 88, 89, 75, 83, 69,
51, 52, 56, 70, 55, 112, 109, 113, 114, 1

Second Makkan: 54, 37, 71, 76, 44, 50, 20, 26,
15, 19, 38, 36, 43, 72, 67, 23, 21, 25, 17, 27, 18

Third Makkan: 32, 41, 45, 16, 30, 11, 14, 12,
40, 28, 39, 29, 31, 42, 10, 34, 35, 7, 46, 6, 13

Madinan: 2, 98, 64, 62, 8, 47, 3, 61, 57, 4, 65,
59, 33, 63, 24, 58, 22, 48, 66, 60, 110, 49,
9 but vv. 12-21 earlier, 5 but parts earlier

This system is not accepted by all scholars, whether Muslim or non-Muslim, but it provides a solid foundation for further exploration of the origins, structure, and interpretation of the Qur'an. Also, the three Makkan periods identified in this system do not correspond directly to the three historical periods of preaching outlined in the above sketch of the Prophet's life. The disagreement between the two schemes can be explained simply as a reflection of our ignorance of what actually took place during the lifetime of the Prophet. In addition to the four periods of revelation listed, the system identifies Makkan additions to other Makkan surahs, Makkan insertions in Madinan surahs, Madinan insertions in Makkan surahs, and additions to Makkan surahs of uncertain date. These variances point to the difficulties associated with studying a complex text like the Qur'an and should serve as a caution against too quickly accepting the results of scholarship, or tradition, as established fact.

The Second Revelation

Nun. By the pen! By all they write! Your Lord's grace does not make you [Prophet] a madman: you will have a never-ending reward — truly you have a noble character — and soon you will see, as will they, which of you is afflicted with madness. (68:1-6)

You [Prophet], enfolded in your cloak! Keep vigil throughout the night, all but a small part of it, half, or a little more; recite the Qur'an slowly and distinctly: We shall send a momentous message down to you. (73:1-5)

You, wrapped in your cloak, arise and give warning!
Proclaim the greatness of your Lord; cleanse yourself; keep
away from all filth; do not be overwhelmed and weaken;
be steadfast in your Lord's cause. (74:1-7)

There is no agreement among scholars as to which one of these three passages, if any, was the literal second revelation. According to traditional accounts, these verses are thought to have come to the Prophet after a period of a few days following the original encounter with Gabriel in the cave, (i.e., following the revelation of the initial verses of surah 96). It should be noted that each of these passages, as with the initial revelation, make up only a small portion (about one quarter) of the text of the surahs in which they are contained. We will examine them in the reverse order to which they appear in the Qur'an.

In surah 74, *Wrapped in his Cloak*, Muhammad is given a series of eight instructions in rapid succession with little accompanying explanation. The initial command to arise might be interpreted to indicate the transition from his state of doubt and fear following the first revelation, to a state of action. The second command to give warning clearly identifies Muhammad as a prophet, as the burden of the call to prophecy within the Abrahamic religious traditions is to warn a particular group of people, who are likely to be unreceptive, that turning away from God will result in divine retribution. The third command provides a counterpoint to the second order inasmuch as the Prophet is also to proclaim the greatness of God. The next two orders

33

refer to the physical and spiritual state of purity that the Prophet must be in, in order to carry out his work, and the following two commands are phrased in the negative indicating that he is not to view his task as too onerous or beyond his capabilities. The final command is for him to be steadfast, not for his own sake, but so that he can carry out God's bidding.

Surah 73, *Enfolded*, begins in a similar manner to surah 74 however, in this case, the Prophet is instructed to spend much of his time in prayer, especially during the night when he can be alone. Unlike the continual string of commands outlined in surah 74, in this instance, the command to pray or keep vigil, receives a series of qualifiers, with respect to exactly how much time the Prophet is to devote to it. This is followed by a command to recite the Qur'an, in other words, an order to constantly repeat the revelations that have come to him. He is to do this slowly and distinctly, as befits the gravity of the message.

Space does not permit a detailed examination of the remaining verses of these two surahs, but some interesting common characteristics should be pointed out. First, the beginnings of these two surahs are remarkably similar, especially in the way they refer to the Prophet (cloaked, enfolded). Some scholars have suggested that all of the surahs in the Qur'an exist in complementary pairs and that the Prophet used to recite the surahs in these pairings during public prayer (Robinson 2003: 272). Second, surahs 73 and 74 each contain what I referred to in the previous chapter as an interpolation – a very long verse that appears inconsistent with the

structural characteristics of the early first Makkan period surahs. One question that arises from this observation is whether these surahs were constructed from
three separate revelations – the first containing the initial verses, the second containing the remaining short
verses, and the third containing a single long verse.

The final verse (20) of surah 73 is about one quarter of the length of the entire surah and appears to be a
later comment on the command to pray and recite the
Qur'an found in the opening verses. In this instance, the
verse acknowledges that the Prophet spends much of
the night praying and reciting, and that this may present a hardship. Consequently, the instruction in this instance is to do only as much "as is easy for you" and that
however much the Prophet does will be improved and
increased. Verse 31 of surah 74 is roughly in the middle
of the surah, and appears to be a later inserted explanation for the contents of verse 30, which states that there
are nineteen guards of hell. Judging by the contents of
verse 31, we might conclude that some hearers of the
message were perplexed by the reference to the number
nineteen. The response given is that this number is a test
for the unbelievers and that those who believe and who
follow the scripture will have nothing to fear, for they
will be guided on the proper path.

The Pen (68) begins with an individual Arabic letter
nun, and proceeds to reassure the Prophet that he is
not mad as many of his opponents suggested. There are
no commands in this sequence, just words of reassur-
ance and the establishment of a contrast between the
Prophet, who will be the recipient of God's reward,

and the opponents, who will soon realize that they are the ones suffering from madness in their denial of God and His messenger. The reference to the pen and writing can been interpreted as a direct link to surah 96, with its message of the pen as the means by which God brings knowledge to humanity, through the Qur'an. The single letter *nun* might serve as a symbol for the written word. Indeed, others could use a pen and produce texts but the Qur'an was a special case, in that it was the revealed word of God.

Looking more closely at some of the remaining verses of surah 68, we find a couple of remarkable passages. The first is a story in the form of a parable (17-33) – a device commonly used in the Gospels by Jesus to teach his disciples. The second is a brief reference to the story of Jonah (48-50). The book of Jonah is among the writings of the twelve Minor Prophets contained in the second major section of the Hebrew Bible known as the *Nevi'im*, or writings of the Prophets. In the story, Jonah is thrown overboard by his fellow crew members. They blame him for putting their lives in danger during a violent storm at sea. He is swallowed by a large fish and remains in the belly of the fish for three days and three nights before being spewed out onto the shore. At this point, he is called by God to bring a warning to the people of Nineveh. In the Qur'an, the details of the story and Jonah's name are not provided.

Both the use of a parable and the telling of the Jonah story provide direct links to the scripture of the Jews and Christians, and yet these surahs are considered to be among the first ones to be revealed. Would the initial audience for these surahs, let alone Muhammad, possess the knowledge necessary to fill in the rest of the details of these stories or make the link back to the previous scriptures? What would be the point of making these sorts of references if in fact the Qur'an was revealed in an environment of idolatry and ignorance? We may never be able to answer such questions, but they do draw attention to the way in which some familiarity with Jewish and Christian scripture can assist the modern reader in approaching the Qur'an.

I end this chapter with a brief examination of another early surah that helps us to further understand the context in which the message of the Qur'an was first received. Not only are the events of this surah situated in the social milieu of Makkah, but also it deals with one of the most important religious themes of the early surahs, namely, judgment.

Palm Fibre

May the hands of Abu Lahab be ruined! May he be ruined too! Neither his wealth nor his gains will help him: he will burn in the Flaming Fire, and so will his wife, the firewood-carrier, with a palm-fibre rope around her neck. (111:1-5)

This short surah contains the only direct (by name) condemnation of an individual (Abu Lahab, an uncle of Muhammad) found in the Qur'an. Abu Lahab, whose name translates roughly as flame-man, based apparently on his temperament as well as his complexion, was a staunch opponent of the Prophet, and his condemnation foreshadows the fate of those who would stand in the way of God and His messenger. This surah also clearly demonstrates how the content of the revelations was often provided in direct response to a challenge faced by Muhammad. Particularly in later surahs, the Qur'an acknowledges its responsive nature more explicitly, as for example in 4:127, where, just before a sequence of verses on the equitable treatment of women, we read: "They ask you [Prophet] for a ruling about women." At the same time, because the initial hearers of the revelation would have known Abu Lahab, and would have been witness to his opposition to the Prophet, there is an air of familiarity and direct relevance to the message of these verses.

Another point of interest regarding this surah is that it also condemns the wife of Abu Lahab, who, according to tradition, was known for her own cruelty against the Prophet – she would bundle thorns together with palm fibre and throw them in Muhammad's path. Through relating the judgment against these two individuals, this early section of the Qur'an appears to be declaring that men and women are equally accountable before God and that opposition to the will and work of God will be punished.

3

Statement of Faith
(Qur'an 1, 112, 114, 24:35)

The Opening

(1) In the name of God, the Lord of Mercy, the Giver of Mercy! (2) Praise belongs to God, Lord of the Worlds, (3) the Lord of Mercy, the Giver of Mercy, (4) Master of the Day of Judgment. (5) It is You we worship; it is You we ask for help. (6) Guide us on the straight path; (7) the path of those You have blessed, those who incur no anger and who have not gone astray. (1:1-7)

This short surah opens the Qur'an and in many ways provides a summary or 'table of contents' for all that follows (Haleem 1999: 21). The importance of this surah in the faith and practice of Islam cannot be overly emphasized. For example, devout Muslims recite this surah at least seventeen times per day as part of their five obligatory prayers. Similarly, this surah is used to seal contracts, to bestow blessings, and to seek the restored health of those who are ill. Following an analysis of the content of these seven verses, I provide a comparison of this surah to the Lord's Prayer and then demonstrate how two of the final surahs of the Qur'an (112 and 114) serve both to conclude and to continue the message of the opening surah. The chapter ends with a brief reflection on the so-called Light verse (24: 35), as a means of providing some insight into the metaphysical and mystical side of Islam.

Invocation (1:1)

The purpose of an invocation is to initiate an action under the authority of someone or something other than oneself, as in the familiar expression: "Stop in the name of the law." In the Qur'an, the invocation, technically known as the *basmalah*, appears as the first numbered verse of this surah and occurs as an un-numbered preface to every other surah with the exception of surah 9, which, as will be explained in the next paragraph, does not begin in the conventional manner. The actual numbering of the verses did not occur until quite recently, and there are still some discrepancies among alternate number schemes (Kassis 1983: xviii). However, the fact that in most editions the invocation is numbered only in the first surah can be interpreted in various ways. It might be meant to imply that the invocation is an integral part of the first surah, while serving as an added preface to all other surahs (Yusuf Ali 2004: 15).

It could also imply that the entire first surah, not just this single verse, serves as an invocation to the Qur'an as a whole, or that to begin each surah with the invocation is in some sense to begin each surah with the entire first surah.

With respect to the omission of the invocation at the beginning of surah 9, several explanations have been offered. One opinion is that the Prophet instructed that this collection of verses be placed after surah 8 but did not make it clear whether they should be treated as comprising a separate surah (Yusuf Ali 2004: 435). Others think that because surah 9 calls upon Muslims to kill the idolaters of Makkah, the recitation of the invocation as a preface to this act would only serve to stress the inconsistency of this action with the more generally preferred behavior of showing mercy (Robinson 2003: 18). It is important to note however, that the invocation does occur 114 times in the Qur'an appearing twice in surah 27. As expected, the first instance is at the beginning of the surah however, it occurs again in verse 30 as part of the story of the Queen of Sheba. In this story, she receives a letter from Solomon that begins with the *basmalah*. One possible interpretation of this particular use of the invocation will be discussed in chapter 5.

In *The Opening*, the Qur'an begins by calling upon the authority of God. When reading the Qur'an, or studying any of the Abrahamic faiths, it must be remembered that the word "God" is not a name; it is a title. The notion of God in Islam as well as in Judaism and Christianity is one of a transcendent and ineffable being. It is a fundamental theological precept

41

of all three of these faiths that God must be beyond description; yet, God can be referred to indirectly by a number of superlatives. For example, if a person can be described as being good, then God must represent the ultimate good. For the purpose of the invocation, it is the quality of mercy in particular that is referred to and God is identified as the Lord of Mercy and the Giver of Mercy. The shift from the title God to the title Lord signals the shift from identifying the divine being as something unknowable and remote to indicating that the deity can be known to some extent through various attributes and actions. Remember that in the earliest surahs, when Islam is not yet firmly established, God is consistently referred to as Lord.

The notion of "Lord" implies someone who is in charge of something, but it also carries with it the idea of stewardship. In other words, lordship entails not only control and command, but also the idea of care and concern for whatever jurisdiction the person, or deity, is lord over (Haleem 1999: 17). Thus, to speak of God in the first instance as "Lord of Mercy" establishes the fact that there is a relationship between God and humanity. Further, it establishes the nature of that relationship: God rules humanity, but God is also concerned for humanity. To refer to God in the second instance as "Giver of Mercy" indicates that God is not remote. Rather, God is actively engaged in an outpouring of mercy upon those creatures who are dependent upon Him and who owe their very existence to Him.

Identification (1:2-4)

These three verses can be viewed as an extension of the invocation, but they also serve to identify God more fully, particularly with respect to the relationship between God and humanity. The first half of verse 2 states that all praise belongs to God, while the second half identifies God as the "Lord of the Worlds". This pairing of phrases is reminiscent of the verbal exchange in the morning and evening prayer services of the Christian Church, in which the minister and congregation recite the following: "Oh Lord open thou our lips, and our mouths shall show forth thy praise." It is common to identify speech and language as the characteristic that separates humans from other animals. In some sense then, the implication of this line from the Christian service as well as the opening phrase of verse 2 of *The Opening* is that, by the very act of speaking, we are praising God. That is, in using this unique capability that God has bestowed upon us, we are engaging in an act of thanks or worship. Thus, in the Qur'an, this phrase recognizes that if it was not for the gift of speech, not only could the invocation not be made, but also all that follows would not exist. Support for this interpretation can be found in the way this phrase is used in everyday life. When you ask Muslims how they are, they reply: "All praise belongs to God."

The second half of verse 2 uses the title "Lord" for "God" and indicates that the jurisdiction of this lordship is the worlds. The word "worlds" in this instance can be interpreted to encompass all of creation or, more specifically, all of humanity (Haleem 1999: 18). In the first instance, God is the lord of everything that exists – even those things that are beyond our comprehension or experience. More directly however, God is the lord of people, sharing a special relationship with them that can be known and articulated by them.

Verse 3 repeats the initial pair of attributes associated with God in verse 1 and thus, serves to reiterate the emphasis on mercy as well as indicate that God's relationship to creation and humanity is defined by mercy. This is particularly important with respect to verse 4, which identifies God as the Master or Lord of the Day of Judgment. Although God will judge and potentially punish those He has created, His first quality is that of mercy. A parallel for this idea can be found in the Christian service of the Mass, where as part of the prayer said just prior to receiving communion, the following words appear: "But thou art the same Lord, Whose property is always to have mercy." In other words, no matter how unworthy people may be, as a result of sin or ignoring their religious obligations, God's first response is always one of mercy. In these few verses, God is identified in four distinct ways (Lord of the Worlds, Lord of Mercy, Giver of Mercy, and Master of the Day of Judgment). These four attributes are among many that are used to refer to God in the Qur'an, and together they belong to a larger group of superlatives that are referred to in Islamic religious thought as the 99 beautiful names of God (7:180). The names are commonly used as part of devotional exercises (Murata and Chittick 1994: 58-59; Chittick 1989:

33-46), and in the Qur'an they perform a number of important functions.

Robinson (2003: 200) indicates that while the term "Lord" is used more than 950 times in the Qur'an with respect to God, this term is never used as part of the poetic structure of the surahs. In contrast, the other names or attributes of God are often used within the rhyme scheme of the verses as a way to reinforce the message through sound, often occurring in related pairs, for example, All-wise, All-knowing (6:83) and the Most Subtle, the All Aware (67:14). He indicates that these names can be sorted into a small number of categories, each reflecting a major characteristic of God. They are: omniscience, omnipotence, benefi-cence, indulgence, uniqueness, perfection, and reliabil-ity. Examples of names representing these attributes which occur several times throughout the Qur'an are: All-knowing (154 times); All-mighty (88 times); All-merciful (115 times); All-forgiving (91 times); Patron (35 times); One (22 times); Self-sufficient (18 times).

Apart from their use to reinforce the message they accompany, Robinson identifies a number of other uses for the names. For example, they are used to mark the ending of a sub-section within a surah; to reinforce a preceding statement; and to guard against misunder-standing. This latter use can be illustrated by verse 2:267, in which God is called Self-sufficient, following instructions about giving offerings to God. The divine name in this instance is used to point out that God has no material needs. Further, the names can be used to provide cohesion to a major section within a surah, such as the use of the pairing of "All-forgiving" and "All-merciful" that occurs six times between verses 153 and 242 in surah 2. Similarly, the names can give cohesion to an entire surah as in the case of the attribute "All-powerful" appearing six times throughout surah 2, in verses 20, 106, 109, 148, 259 and 283. Finally, the names are used to provide a linkage between two or more non-adjacent subsections. In other words, they provide continuity in instances where themes recur or a story continues at a number of places within a surah, often separated by distinctly different material. Thus, the pairing of "Oft-relenting" and "All-merciful" occurs in verses 37, 54, 128 and 160 of surah 2, and in only five other places in the Qur'an. We will examine some of these linkages in chapter 9, which is devoted to surah 2.

Affirmation (1:5)

An affirmation is a statement of acknowledgement, acceptance, or agreement. In this instance, the object or receiver of the affirmation is God. In surah 1 verse 5, two separate things are being affirmed; the first being that God is the object of human worship and the second, that it is God whom humans ask for help. Both statements affirm humanity's reliance on God and suggest that without God, humans are incomplete. It is important in this verse that worship precedes the request for assistance. In other words, God comes before humanity and in recognition of God's place in the grand order of things; praising God takes precedence over asking God for anything. From a structural point of view, the word worship is a direct link back to the word praise in verse 2, and the notion of asking for help is linked directly to the word guide in verse 6. Thus, the distribution of key words in this surah reinforces the centrality of this verse as the core message of the surah.

In the previous sections, I separated the invocation (verse 1) from the identification (verses 2 to 4) for analytical purposes. In essence, and certainly with respect to the affirmation (verse 5), the first four verses of the opening surah should be taken together as a unit. In this way, the surah as a whole demonstrates what is known as a chiastic structure, where both outer parts (verses 1-4 and 6-7) point inward towards the central message contained in verse 5. This literary device was used extensively in the Torah (Breck 1994; Welch 1981) and, as I attempt to demonstrate throughout this text, it is used to powerful effect in the Qur'an.

The notion of a chiasm is based on the way in which a scribe would draw the Greek letter X, starting at the top left and moving the pen down and forward to the bottom right and then going to the bottom left and moving the pen up and forward to the upper right. Applying this idea to a text, the reader has the sensation that whether they start from the beginning or from the end of a text, their attention is drawn towards a common midpoint which conveys the principle message of the passage they are reading.

invocation (1-4)   praise – rising up

affirmation (5)

petition (6-7)   seeking guidance –
                        calling down

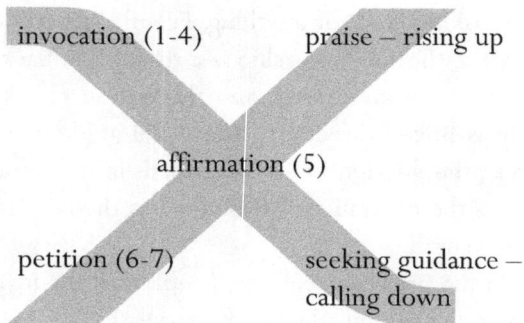

In *The Opening*, the chiastic element is even further emphasized by the fact that the content and structure of the text complement each other in a way that completes the crossover. So, while the structure of the invocation leads down to the first part of the affirmation, it can also be viewed as a rising up of people's voices towards God. Similarly, while the structure of the petition points upward to the second part of the affirmation, it also denotes a calling down of God's mercy, which will comprise of guidance. This pairing of themes illustrates the dual nature of the Qur'an. Not only is it a manual of praise, providing the words that will be recited by the faithful in their acts of worship, it is also a book of guidance for those who will study it and learn from it how they are to live their lives.

Petition (1:6-7)

A petition might be viewed as a simple request but there is the implication of an unequal distribution of power in the word petition. Thus, I do not petition my children to pick up their toys, but I do petition the government or some other authority structure for example, when I make a request as a citizen to have my concerns addressed. The single request made of God (by people reciting this surah) is to be guided on the straight path. This path is identified as the one that people who have received God's blessings in the past have followed. The petitioners also state their awareness of the fact that in the past, some people have incurred anger and gone astray. In other words, the verse recognizes that some members of previous generations have not responded to God's blessings.

The Lord's Prayer

Here is the Lord's Prayer as it appears in the New Jerusalem Bible (one of many popular translations):

Our Father, Who art in heaven,
Hallowed be Thy name,
Thy kingdom come
Thy will be done, on earth as it is in heaven
Give us this day our daily bread, and forgive us our debts
As we forgive those to whom we are indebted
Lead us not into temptation and deliver us from evil.
(Matthew 6:9-14)

As Haleem (1999: 24) points out, a number of Christian scholars have compared the opening surah of the Qur'an with the Lord's Prayer, often with the intention of showing the indebtedness of Islam to Christianity. While this is certainly not my intention, the Lord's Prayer, which has its origins in the Gospels, is worth exploring as part of our discussion because it is the most commonly recited prayer among Christians of all denominations. As background to what follows, it is important to recognize that while Muslims would hold the view that there is nothing in *The Opening* that could be considered inappropriate for recitation by either Christians or Jews, the Lord's Prayer contains a number of references that would not be acceptable to Muslims. Members of all three Abrahamic faiths could recite *The Opening*, because all three faiths share the same God, and because there is nothing in *The Opening* that can be considered doctrinally specific to Islam. In other words, *The Opening* is consistent with the theology of all three faiths. Even though both prayers are directed to the same God and contain the same basic components (invocation, affirmation, petition), there are a number of differences with respect to the origin, content and context of these prayers that are worth noting (Haleem 1999: 24-27).

To begin with, we possess the text of *The Opening* in the original Arabic, while we only have the Lord's Prayer in Greek. Biblical scholars agree that the original language of the prayer that Jesus taught his disciples was Aramaic, and even though many attempts have been made to translate the prayer back into its original language, scholars are unanimous in their agreement that any such effort will at best result in an unverifiable approximation. Furthermore, there are two versions of the Lord's Prayer, the most familiar one that is found in Matthew (6:9-14) and a shorter version in Luke (11:2-4). *The Opening* was placed at the beginning of the Qur'an and all Muslims around the world, irrespective of their native language, have said the prayer in the same way since the inception of Islam. This serves both to reinforce the primacy of Arabic, the language of the Qur'an, and to remind Muslims everywhere and at all times that they are part of one community of faith. The Lord's Prayer came about in response to a question from the disciples of Jesus about how they should pray in order to distinguish themselves from others who also prayed to God. Today, the Lord's Prayer is recited in the many vernacular languages of Christians all over the world.

With respect to points that Muslims would find objectionable in the Lord's Prayer, the first is that the invocation begins with the expression "Our Father." This statement might be interpreted to imply that somehow God is exclusive to a certain group, and that God is a parent. Both of these ideas are contrary to the Islamic notion of the Oneness of God, which not only implies that there is only one universal deity but that otherness cannot be attributed to God. As was outlined above with respect to the names of God in the Qur'an, attributes such as forgiveness, when they are attributed to God, are used in the superlative rather than the comparative sense; that is, they are beyond human attainment. Generally, God cannot be seen to have children or display any human characteristics. Further, the petition portion of the Lord's Prayer contains a number of specific requests – for daily bread, for forgiveness, and for safety from being led into temptation. The first of these might be interpreted as mundane and selfish, while the second request appears to make humans an example for God to follow. As it is stated in the Lord's Prayer, petitioners ask God to forgive them their trespasses as they forgive people who trespass against them.

Purity [of Faith]

Say, 'He is God the One, God the eternal. He fathered no one nor was He fathered. No one is comparable to Him. (112:1-4)

This very short surah can be viewed as the theological conclusion of the Qur'an. It is not the last surah in the Qur'an, but it provides a summary statement of the overarching theme of the Oneness of God presented in *The Opening* and thus, draws to a close the various lessons and examples contained in the intervening surahs. At the same time, based on the discussion in the previous section, it may be interpreted as a condemnation of Christianity, particularly with respect to the doctrine of the Trinity, which might appear (to some) to suggest that the Father, the Son (Jesus), and the Holy Spirit are three equal and distinct deities.

Scholars and Church officials who were dealing with the emergence of a number of heretical sects established the notion of the Trinity as part of Christian doctrine in the early part of the fourth century. Their answer was to create a unified statement of faith to which all Christians must adhere, thereby declaring both their orthodoxy and their allegiance to the authority of the Church. The creed, or statement of faith, begins with the line: "I believe in One God, the Father Almighty,

Maker of heaven and earth, and of all things visible and invisible." Consistent with the Lord's Prayer, God is referred to as Father, and consistent with the fundamental tenet of all three Abrahamic faiths, God is referred to as One. At the same time, God is described as the creator of all things. Later in the creed, we read that Jesus was "begotten not made, being of one substance with the Father through whom all things were made." The precise theological interpretation of this statement has been debated since the time it was written. However, surah 112 suggests that this element of Christian doctrine is unacceptable within Islam. At the same time, it is important to point out that a condemnation of the doctrines of the Christian Church is not necessarily equivalent to a condemnation of Christianity. In contrast to the creed, surah 112 bears a striking resemblance to one of the most common prayers of Judaism, the *shema* or "hearing."

The *shema* is found in the Torah, in the sixth chapter of the book of Deuteronomy (6:4) and it begins: "Hear, O Israel, the Lord your God, the Lord is One." As in *The Opening*, God is identified in the *shema* as Lord, and as with surah 112, God is identified as One. However, there are two differences worth noting. First, in contrast to surah 112 and much of the rest of the Qur'an, the instruction in the *shema* is to hear rather than to say. This reflects the fact that it was the Jewish priests and elders who regularly read scripture to the faithful. Second, the intended listener is the nation of Israel – the chosen people, rather than all people. Judaism was established as a religion and a way of life for a particular group of people who entered into a covenant with God and were promised prosperity in exchange for adherence to God's law. Islam on the other hand was established as a universal religion, revealed in the first instance to the Arabs, but meant for everyone for all time.

People

> *Say, 'I seek refuge with the Lord of people, the Controller of people, the God of people, against the evil of the slinking whisperer — who whispers into the hearts of people — whether they be jinn or people.'* (114:1-6)

This final surah of the Qur'an is linked in content to some extent with surah 113 (*Daybreak*) yet, if surah 112 draws the Qur'an to a theological close, how can we explain the existence of these two short surahs that appear to be added on to the main body of the text? In both of the final surahs the reader is seeking refuge from evil and, while both surahs are often used by Muslims as prayers to ward off evil, there is particular significance to the final surah. It performs at least four very important functions with respect to the rest of the Qur'an. First, through its references to God, Lord and Controller (or Master), it reiterates the invocation portion of *The Opening*, thus indicating that from the perspective of religious practice it is correctly placed as the final surah. Second, by linking the word "people" with the attributes of God, it makes clear that the religion explained throughout the Qur'an, not to mention the text of the Qur'an itself, is for the guidance of people. The use of the word "people," which is absent from *The Opening*, cannot be overemphasized. The first surah makes clear the point that praise is due to God and, while all of creation bears witness to God, it is only people, through the gift of speech, who are able to praise God and seek God's mercy. I discuss the jinn in chapter 8. God is the Master of the Day of Judgment and it is people to whom this day is relevant. Third, this surah draws a sharp contrast between the clear message of the Qur'an, which is to be recited aloud, and the hushed tones of the "slinking whisperer," both of which stir the hearts of people. Finally, because this surah provides such a strong thematic link to the opening surah of the Qur'an, it serves as reminder that recitation has not ended. Rather, braced against evil, one now returns to the beginning and starts again.

The Light Verse

God is the Light of the heavens and earth. (24:35)

This brief statement begins one of the best-known and most evocative verses in the Qur'an. Unlike the passages we have examined so far, which employ relatively straightforward language to convey fundamental aspects of Islamic beliefs and practices, the "Light verse" makes use of imagery and metaphor to provide insight into the more mystical and spiritual dimensions of Islam. At the same time, through this use of light as a means of expressing God's glory, the Qur'an is demonstrating its coherence and consistency with the scripture of the Jews and Christians.

In the Torah, God's first communication with Moses is through a burning bush (Exodus 3:2). At a later point, after Moses has spent forty days on the mountain receiving the Law from God, his face radiates (Exodus 34:29), such that the people are afraid to approach him. In the Gospel of John, Jesus is often described in terms of light, as in 1:3-4, where we read: "What came to be through him was life, and this life was the light of the human race; the light shines in the darkness, and the darkness has not overcome it." Elsewhere (John 9:5), Jesus says to his disciples: "While I am in the world, I am the light of the world."

In all three traditions, light and the process of illumination are used as a means to convey the dispelling of ignorance and the refreshment of the human spirit that can only come about as a result of being exposed to, and being open to, the radiance of God (Murata and Chittick 1994: 87-89). Similarly, in all three religions, but especially in Islam, as many passages from the Qur'an illustrate (e.g., 13:16, 33:43, 113:1) God's relationship to humanity and the rest of the created order is often described in terms of a contrast between light and dark. To the extent that people and all aspects of creation reflect the light of God, they in a sense come to resemble God or represent God – they are enlightened, and like God, they can share that light with others who are open to it (Mulla Sadra 2004). By contrast, darkness represents difference (otherness) and incomparability to God.

In reading the "Light verse," it is evident that, even in translation, the words of the Qur'an can be beautiful and elegant, stirring in the reader a genuine sense of wonder and awe at what has been preserved for us in this scripture. It is far too easy, when so much effort is being expended on dissecting and analyzing the text, to lose sight of the fact that the Qur'an is first and foremost a divine guidebook. Whether Muslim or not, it is my conviction that, to the extent that the reader approaches the text from this perspective, the greater the level of understanding he or she will gain from their efforts.

4

Joseph
(Qur'an 12)

In comparison to the rest of the surahs in the
Qur'an, *Joseph* (12) provides a remarkable counter-
example to readers' expectations with respect to
the thematic and structural unity that it displays; that
is, it appears to be a 'chapter' in the conventional sense
of the term. The Joseph story is well known among
Jews, Christians, and Muslims, and it has become a
well-established component of popular culture around
the world. It is the longest continuous narrative in the
Hebrew Bible, taking up about one quarter of the book
of Genesis, and it is the longest, and arguably the only
continuous narrative in the Qur'an at about 100 verses
in length. While the stories of Moses and other prophets in the Qur'an are scattered throughout numerous
surahs, apart from two passing references to his name

in other places (6:84, 40:34), the story of Joseph is confined to the surah that bears his name. For readers new to the Qur'an, this surah provides an excellent entry point for the exploration of an extended passage, and it serves as a means to draw attention to some broader characteristics of the way in which the Qur'an is structured. Also, as the sections below will demonstrate, it is one of the few portions of the Qur'an for which there is a substantial analytical literature available in English (e.g., Haleem 1999: 138-57; Kaltner 2003; MacDonald 1956; Morris 1994; Stern 1985).

Among other things, especially for those who are familiar with the story of Joseph found in Genesis, this surah helps us to understand how the accounts of the prophets and personalities presented in the Qur'an differ from the versions we find in the scripture of the Jews and Christians. It also provides us with an excellent opportunity for analyzing the Qur'an as a literary work, illustrating how devices such as characterization, dialogue, the use of time and so on, are used to establish and reinforce the overall message of the Qur'an. Further, it demonstrates how the text of the Qur'an responds to the needs of Muhammad and the growing Islamic community and how individual story units are integrated into the text as a whole through the use of prologues, epilogues and linking passages.

Given the amount of detail provided, and the relative length of continuous text presented in this surah, it might seem logical to assume that both Muhammad and those who first heard this surah were already quite familiar with the story of Joseph. For one thing, there is no reason to think that this story enjoyed any less popularity then, than it does now, even in the absence of modern media. Similarly, given the amount of space devoted to the story in Genesis, even a passing introduction to the Torah, perhaps from a Jewish trader in Makkah, would have likely included mention of Joseph. We have no adequate means of determining whether any of these ideas reflect reality at the time of the Prophet, but it does highlight again the debate over whether the context for the revelation of the Qur'an was one of pagan idolatry or competing monotheisms. Whatever the situation was fourteen centuries ago, I think it is fair to suggest, at least with respect to contemporary readers, that the more familiar they are with the Genesis account of this story, the more they are likely to get out of the version found in surah 12.

This chapter is divided into four sections, with the final one containing a brief analysis of the prologue and epilogue portions of the surah along with some reflections on the context of the surah within the Qur'an. The remaining three sections provide an outline of alternate, but complementary, approaches to the study of this surah, namely, dramatic analysis, literary analysis, and comparative analysis (Qur'an and Torah).

Dramatic Analysis

Simply put, a dramatic analysis treats the text as if it was written as a play, with a series of spoken interchanges between specified characters taking place in a variety of settings. At the same time, as A.H. Johns

(2004: 218) suggests, treating the text as a play allows us to gain at least some appreciation of the oral character of the Qur'an, even in translation. It further helps us to understand the complex interplay between what is being said and the situation in which speaking takes place, in a way that it is attentive to natural speech patterns and turns of phrase.

The Joseph story combines report and dialogue to relate a complicated series of events, and along with the narrator there are no less than seventeen speaking parts as follows: Jacob and his attendants, Joseph, Joseph's brothers together, two of the brothers individually (the brothers are not named), the water-drawer, the Egyptian governor and his wife, the witness, the women of the city, the two prisoners, the King of Egypt and his ministers, the crier, and the pursuers. In this surah, the King of Egypt is not referred to as Pharaoh, perhaps to avoid confusion with the Pharaoh who ruled Egypt at the time of Moses and who plays a prominent role throughout the Qur'an. Only two of the many characters are actually named in the Qur'an – Jacob and Joseph, and while Abraham and Isaac are named in the surah, they are clearly not characters in the drama. Reporting is done by the narrator and in several places, a group of characters act like the chorus in Greek tragedy, expressing their agreement on an issue or indicating what might pass as the accepted view (so-called 'common sense') on some point or other. Johns (2004: 220-39) divides the story into eleven separate acts (indicated by Roman numerals with the appropriate verses in brackets) based on the location in which the action is taking place. Each act is further divided into a varying number of distinct scenes corresponding to which characters are engaged in dialogue. The entire speech structure of the surah is as follows:

Act I (4-21) – Jacob's home in Canaan
    Sc. 1 – Joseph and Jacob
    Sc. 2 – Joseph's brothers together, two brothers
    Sc. 3 – Joseph's brothers and Jacob
    Sc. 4 – Joseph in the well
    Sc. 5 – Joseph's brothers and Jacob
Act II (19-22) – Joseph enters Egypt
    Sc. 1 – water-drawer
    Sc. 2 – Egyptian governor and his wife
Act III (23-34) – governor's house
    Sc. 1 – governor's wife and Joseph
    Sc. 2 – governor, his wife, Joseph, and witness
    Sc. 3 – women
    Sc. 4 – governor's wife, Joseph, and women
Act IV (35-42) – prison
    Sc. 1 – Joseph and two prisoners
Act V (43-57) – King's court
    Sc. 1 – King, ministers, and cupbearer
    Sc. 2 – Joseph and cupbearer
    Sc. 3 – King and Joseph
    Sc. 4 – King, women, governor's wife
    Sc. 5 – Joseph
        Scenes 3 through 5 – cupbearer as intermediary
    Sc. 6 – King and Joseph
Act VI (58-62) – Joseph's home

Sc. 1 – Joseph and his brothers

Act VII (63-68) – Jacob's home in Canaan

Sc. 1 – Joseph's brothers and Jacob

Act VIII (68-79) – Joseph's home and environs

Sc. 1 – Joseph and his younger brother

Sc. 2 – crier, brothers, and pursuers

Sc. 3 – brothers and Joseph

Act IX (80-87) – Jacob's home in Canaan

Sc. 1 – oldest brothers, brothers, and Jacob

Act X (88-93) – Joseph's home

Sc. 1 – brothers and Joseph

Act XI (94-101) – Jacob's journey and Joseph's home

Sc. 1 – Jacob and his attendants

Sc. 2 – Jacob and brothers

Sc. 3 – Joseph

For purposes of illustration, only a few key sequences from the 28 separate scenes identified by Johns will be examined in more detail.

Scene 4 of Act I (when Joseph is alone in the well) is comprised of a single verse (15), which states: "You will tell them of all this [at a time] when they do not realize [who you are]!" This revelation can be interpreted as showing the reader that God is with Joseph and that he will inherit the mantle of prophecy from his father Jacob, as well as indicating that the events that are about to take place are being directed by God, not by chance or by human will.

The two scenes of Act II provide an interesting contrast. In the first scene, an individual sent to draw water discovers Joseph and his exclamation "It's a boy!" expresses joy and surprise, as if to indicate that this is a chance occurrence with no deeper meaning. In the second scene, where the Egyptian governor is discussing Joseph with his wife, he indicates in rapid sequence that Joseph should be treated well, that he might be of use to them, and that they should adopt him as a son. Not only does this speech provide a stark contrast in terms of pacing, emotion and content to that of the water-drawer, but also it foreshadows the important role that the governor and his wife are about to play in the unfolding of the story.

Scenes 3 through 5 of Act V all make use of an intermediary (the cupbearer) in order to compress time and avoid repetition of content. In the first part of Scene 3, we do not hear what the cupbearer relates to the King but simply that, as a result of what he has heard, he issues an order to have Joseph brought before him. In what follows, we do not hear what the cupbearer says to Joseph, but that Joseph poses a question to the King as a condition of his obedience to the order to come before him. In Scene 4, the intervening dialogue is missing and we move directly to the questioning of the women and the admission of guilt by the governor's wife. In the fifth scene, we are again excluded from hearing the conversations that take place, but instead we are presented with Joseph's explanation of why it was necessary to hear the confession from the governor's wife before he would leave prison. As Johns (2004: 229) points out, some early commentators have suggested that Joseph needed to demonstrate his innocence before engaging in any further activity with Egyptians. Others have suggested that because

Joseph had shown weakness when he asked the cup-bearer (who was released from prison earlier) to mention him to the King, instead of wholly relying on God, he (Joseph) did not immediately respond to the order to leave prison. The implication of this is that Joseph did not want the order for his release to be interpreted as an act of charity on the part of the King. From a dramatic point of view, the time compression (skipping over dialogue and events that we know have taken place) serves to quicken the pace of the action, and the lack of repetition helps us to focus on the critical events within the story. At the same time, Joseph's refusal to comply with the King's order causes a break in the pacing that serves to emphasize the importance of the declaration of innocence.

Act VIII takes place in Joseph's home and the surrounding area. In the first scene, Joseph expresses his love for his younger brother and assures him that the future will not be like the past. This intimate exchange makes the events of the next scene appear all the more startling. The second scene has a large cast, with Joseph's brothers, a band of pursuers, and the crier, who finds Joseph's cup among the youngest brother's belongings. The tension and confusion of this scene are brought out through the use of exchanges between alternate choruses, with the crier establishing the major points of the story. In the third scene, the brothers place their younger brother in the same category as Joseph. That is, they now view their younger brother as a thief, and thus as a threat to them. Whereas they had previously thought of Joseph as robbing them of their birthright, they now see their youngest brother as not only stealing an object from Joseph, but also compromising their future well-being. Through a comment clearly addressed to the reader (audience), Joseph emphasizes how the brothers' remarks understate the real significance of the present situation. This aside not only reinforces that Joseph is in control of what is going on, but it foreshadows the completion of the prophecy of the Act I, Scene 4 that he would tell them of these things at a time when they did not know who he was. At the same time, the brothers demonstrate that they are taking their pledge to God seriously, when one of them offers himself as a substitute for his youngest brother.

Act X consists of a single scene. The brothers, who are still unaware of Joseph's identity, are concerned to secure the release of their youngest brother and to acquire corn, but Joseph jolts them by asking them what they had done in the past. This action fulfills the prophecy from the beginning of the story that he would tell them of their crime when they least expected it. The brothers realize that the man before them is Joseph, and he forgives them, taking on the prophetic dignity that has characterized much of Jacob's speech throughout the story. Joseph avoids making a direct condemnation of his brothers by suggesting that, when they carried out their plan against him, they were in a state of ignorance. The brothers make a direct plea on religious grounds, suggesting that through his actions Joseph is demonstrating that God rewards those who are generous.

Dramatic analysis helps us see the text from the perspective of a listener rather than just a reader. It also helps us to see more clearly the way in which specific aspects of the composition of this surah reinforce the major themes of the story. With particular reference to the story of Joseph, the sophisticated composition of this story might appear to support the idea that the original hearers of this part of the Qur'an were already familiar with the story and thus were in a position to recognize quite easily the specific emphasis that the revelation was designed to draw out.

Literary Analysis

Mustansir Mir (2004a: 381) suggests that the traditional emphasis on the Qur'an as a sacred and primarily theological text has obscured the appreciation of its merits as a literary masterpiece. Some might argue that if the Qur'an is perfect in its content and the beauty of its construction, then analyzing it in the same way as one would a poem or other piece of human artistry would be tantamount to critiquing the literary skills of God. From a more pragmatic position, we might suggest that if the Qur'an is intended to be read by people, it will be structured in such a way as to reflect the normal array of literary devices that people will be familiar with – namely, metaphor, irony, imagery and so on. Of course, one of the problems with trying to discuss these aspects of word play is that, for the most part, we learn to use them in everyday speech, long before we ever formally learn their technical meanings and then attempt to apply them to the analysis of texts.

For present purposes, I want to remind readers of the definition of irony.

According to Chris Baldick (2001), verbal irony "involves a discrepancy between what is said and what is really meant" (114). Dramatic irony involves a situation where the audience knows more about a character's situation than the character does, and thus can foresee an outcome that is contrary to the character's expectations (what might be called a reversal of fortune). Recalling the story of Abu Lahab (surah 111, discussed in chapter 2), it is ironic, for example, that "flame man" is destined to go up in flames.

Mir (2004a) is particularly struck by the deep irony of the Joseph story, as it is related in Genesis and in surah 12, through which "the evil intended by human beings is turned into good by God" (384). He suggests that the Joseph story is not tragic, as there are no losers, but that the events and speech of the story – as they are related in the Qur'an – are used to drive home two important points. The first being that God does not abandon those who place their trust in Him, and the second, that those who have committed wrongs are given an opportunity to correct their mistakes. With respect to the first point, even though Jacob appears to lose Joseph, for example, and even though Joseph finds himself forgotten in prison, father and son are eventually reunited. Joseph is raised to a lofty position, both in earthly terms and in terms of inheriting the mantle of prophecy from Jacob. On the second point, the brothers play out a sequence of parallel events first with Joseph and then with their youngest brother. Through the repetition of these events, their relationship with their father and with their estranged brothers (Joseph and the youngest), and ultimately with God, is perfected.

Turning to another aspect of the literary character of the story, readers cannot help but be struck by the way in which Joseph's shirt is pivotal in three separate episodes. The first instance (verse 18) is when his bloodied shirt is presented to Jacob as proof that a wolf has eaten him. Jacob recognizes that the shirt is not torn, thus calling into question the brothers' account of what happened. The second episode (verse 25) is with reference to the accusation of seduction brought against Joseph by the Egyptian governor's wife. In the third instance (verse 93), Joseph gives his shirt to his brothers and tells them to take it to Jacob as proof that he is alive. The shirt cures Jacob's blindness.

The second episode is particularly striking. It calls to mind the kind of forensic detail that we would associate with the sophisticated crime dramas that we are now accustomed to. The clarity and logic of the argument, as well as the matter-of-fact way in which it is presented, provide a stark contrast to the image of the attempted seduction. The explanation makes sense when we hear it, but how many of us would have thought of it on the spur of the moment? As Ghazali (2000) comments:

> There was no video or voice recording, and no material evidence to support either claim, but the circumstantial evidence was overwhelmingly in Joseph's favor. Simple logic and common sense

pointed to the fact that since his shirt was torn from the back, Joseph must have been innocent. Such circumstantial evidence is admissible in Islamic courts, and so is that obtained through analysis of fingerprints, blood samples and other modern forensic techniques. (239)

This observation demonstrates just how extraordinary the legal proof of Joseph's innocence is viewed to be by commentators.

By comparison, Yusuf Ali relates that due to the nature of alleged events there were no eyewitnesses, but in the furor that resulted, the whole household would have assembled to see what had happened. He suggests that, in instances like this, wisdom comes not to the excited but to those who remain calm. Specifically, in this case, tradition relates that it was a child who offered the explanation. Yusuf Ali (2004), explains this tradition by observing that: "Wisdom comes often through the mouths of babes and sucklings" (554). This last expression, of course, is an appeal to a common scriptural basis for the explanation, as this well-known saying first appears in Psalms 8:2 and is repeated in Matthew 21:16.

Comparative Analysis (Qur'an and Torah)

In his thematic comparison of the Joseph story, as it appears in Genesis and in the Qur'an, Haleem (1999: 138) stresses the fact that the story serves different functions within Judaism and Islam, and that Jews and Muslims have differing intentions in relating this story. Thus, the choice of material and the treatment of various elements of the story are different in each case. For the Jews, the story of Joseph explains the migration of the Hebrew people into Egypt, and sets the stage for the recounting of their subsequent enslavement and eventual release with the selection by the God of Moses as deliverer. Thus, for example, it was important for the names of all those who went down into Egypt to be recorded in Genesis, so that future generations could trace their lineage back to this pivotal event. For Muslims, the story is not about history but about the edification of Muhammad and the believers, to give them strength and guidance through the example of the trials and tribulations of the previous prophets. Thus, specifications of exact names, precise times and locations, and exact quantities of people, livestock, and goods do not appear in the Qur'an.

In Genesis 39:12, Joseph drops his shirt and flees from the Egyptian governor's wife. The ripping of the shirt from behind and the story of the women who cut their hands appear only in the Qur'an. The inclusion of the other women perhaps demonstrates that there was nothing exceptionally sinful about the governor's wife and that any woman would have been tempted by this "precious angel" (12:31). The ripping of the shirt is necessary to provide a basis for establishing innocence in a way that is clear to all. This can be contrasted with the fact that when the wolf supposedly killed Joseph, his shirt was not torn.

Joseph is a prophet, taking over the role from his father Jacob. In Genesis, Jacob and Joseph are patriarchs, ancestors in the bloodline of those to whom

God promised a special land in which their descendants would live and prosper. Joseph does have the ability to interpret dreams in both accounts, but because of his status as a prophet within Islam, it is necessary that his innocence be declared.

In Genesis 43:14, Jacob mentions God only once with reference to the brothers and the man (who turns out to be Joseph) who gives leave to let Joseph and his younger brother go free. As noted by Haleem (1999: 152), in the Qur'an Jacob constantly mentions God, as does Joseph, and together they state in several places that all their hope and trust is placed in God (verses 6, 18, 21, 24, 38, 56, 64, 67, 83, 98 and 101).

Context

As mentioned earlier, it is common in the Qur'an for core sections of the surahs to be bracketed by a small number of verses that present a broader context or complementary lesson for the themes addressed within the surahs. In the case of *Joseph*, in addition to the central story, there is a prologue (1-3), an interpolation (verse 7), and an epilogue (102-111). The first two verses of the prologue deal with the Qur'an. If we assume that people would already be familiar with the Joseph story, then the purpose of mentioning the Qur'an at the outset may be to indicate that through reading the Qur'an people will gain a new understanding of this story. Verse 3 is addressed to Muhammad, and provides a clear link to the previous surah (*Hud*), where we read: "We have told you the stories of the

73

prophets to make your heart firm" (11:120). The point is also made that before this revelation the Prophet knew nothing about these stories. Rather than interpreting this statement literally, it might be more appropriate to interpret it as suggesting that Muhammad was previously unaware of the meaning and significance of the stories.

Verses 4 through 6, which appear to comprise the first part of the central story, recount Joseph's telling of his dream to his father Jacob and his father warning him not to tell his brothers. This incident foreshadows the events that follow, but does not necessarily belong to the temporal order of the rest of the story. In other words, this dream incident could have taken place years or days before the main sequence of events that are about to be related. In fact, the dream sequence has broader significance for the role of Joseph in the history of the Jews and Muslims, and does not provide the basis for the plot by his brothers to eliminate him as is presented from verse 8 onwards. Thus, verse 7 can be viewed as an interpolation, or break in the continuity of the story, that acts as a deliberate signal to the reader to treat the dream material differently from what is to follow. The suggestion in the verse that there are important lessons to be learned by those who seek them may indicate that real understanding will come from looking beyond the literal elements of the story.

The epilogue has four parts, beginning in verse 102 with a link back to verse 3 reiterating that Muhammad was previously not aware of the story. The second part (103-08) tells the Prophet that he cannot make

people believe. The unstated premise here is: "In spite
of stories like this..." This part goes on to explain that
many people will want to attribute partners to God,
for which they will be punished. The third part of the
epilogue (109-10) refers to the difficulties faced by
previous prophets and relates how God helps whom-
ever He pleases. The fourth part (111) contains two
related phrases. The first phrase states: "There is a lesson in the stories of such people for those who understand" (12:111). This is a clear reference back to verse
7 and thus serves to integrate the central story of the
surah with the lessons of the bracketing verses. The
final phrase links the Joseph story to the mention of the
Qur'an in the opening verses, stating that the revelation is a guide and a blessing for those who believe.

According to Islamic tradition (Johns 2004: 240),
the circumstances of revelation for this surah describe
a group of Muhammad's opponents questioning him
saying: "If you are a prophet, tell how Jacob and his
family went from Canaan to Egypt." Even though the
entire Joseph story can be viewed as constituting the
response to this question, the key part of the answer
is given in verse 99: "Welcome to Egypt: you will all
be safe here, God willing." In order to understand the
central importance of this statement, it is instructive to
think about the possible responses to the question, as
well as the motivation for asking this particular question in the first place.

On one hand, we might conclude that the best way
for Muhammad to prove that he was a prophet would
be for him to relate an extraordinary event from the

life of a previous prophet, specifically one from the Torah. We might further suggest that the importance of this question from Muhammad's opponents takes on greater significance because of the number of times that the story of Moses and his struggles with Pharaoh are mentioned in the Qur'an (see the next chapter). In other words, the real intention behind the question about Jacob might actually be for Muhammad to demonstrate why the story of Moses is so important. Clearly, if the sons of Jacob had not gone down into Egypt, then Moses could not have been called by God to deliver their descendants from oppression. Through Joseph, God delivers the Hebrew people to safety in Egypt, and then later when Pharaoh has turned against these people, God uses Moses to deliver them to the safety of the Law and the Promised Land.

5

Moses
(Qur'an 26, 27, 28)

As with the previous chapter, this one is devoted to another individual who is well known to Jews, Christians, and Muslims alike. And, as was the case with Joseph, Moses appears to receive exceptional treatment in the Qur'an. For Joseph it was the extended narrative, while for Moses, it is the fact that he is mentioned by name far more than any other person in the Qur'an (136 times). Even a casual reading of the Qur'an will demonstrate clearly that Muhammad is referred to more often than anyone else, but there are actually only four instances where he is called by name (3:144, 33:40, 47:2, 48:29). The fact that the Prophet is referred to constantly throughout the Qur'an should come as no surprise, as he is the designated recipient of the revelation. What is more curious is why the name of Moses should occur so often, especially if we subscribe to the idea that those hearing the revelation would primarily be Arab polytheists.

On the assumption that the Arabs were fairly familiar with the monotheistic traditions, possibly through their interactions with Jewish and Christian merchants in Makkah and elsewhere, one potential answer to this question is that, after hearing the message of the Qur'an, it would be natural for them to ask why they should not just follow the Law of Moses and become Jews. After all, Moses had brought the message of the One God to the Hebrew people, and many Arabs had been assimilated into the Jewish tribes that were well established in Yathrib and elsewhere in Arabia. Why did the Arabs need a new religion at all? The material covered in this chapter is meant to demonstrate, at least in part, how the Qur'an provides an answer for this question. I begin with an examination of how Moses is dealt with in the scripture of the Jews and Christians.

Moses in the Torah

At several places in the Qur'an (e.g., 3:48, 5:66, 9:111, 57:27), the Torah and the Gospels, as well as the Psalms of David, are identified as the books of God that precede the Qur'an. The Torah, which consists of the so-called Five Books of Moses (Genesis, Exodus, Leviticus, Numbers and Deuteronomy), forms the first part of the Hebrew Bible (what Christians refer to as the Old Testament) and constitutes the key source of Jewish sacred, legal and social tradition.

The book of Genesis provides an account of the creation of the universe and everything in it, establishes the sanctity of the Sabbath, traces the history of key individuals (Adam, Eve, Noah, Abraham, Sarah, Hagar, Isaac, Ishmael and Jacob), and ends with the story of Joseph and the migration of the Hebrew people into Egypt. The book of Exodus picks up the history of the Hebrews a few hundred years later when Joseph has been forgotten and the descendants of Jacob find themselves in bondage, carrying out building projects for Pharaoh. This book contains an account of the early life of Moses, his call to do God's work, his encounter with Pharaoh, the delivery of the Hebrew people out of Egypt, the giving of the Law (Exodus 20:1-17), and the construction of the Tent of Meeting (precursor of the temple in Jerusalem) and the Ark of the Covenant (built to carry the stone tablets on which the Law was inscribed).

The book of Leviticus provides instructions for the performance of sacrifices and the selection and duties of the priests (males from the tribe of Levi) who perform them. It also covers the laws and regulations which were to govern the daily lives of the Hebrew people, with respect to marriage, divorce, dietary regulations (e.g., the prohibition against eating pork, 11:6-7), inheritance and so on. The book of Numbers deals with various attempts to subvert the authority of Moses, either for personal gain, or in an effort to return to a more secure and comfortable life in Egypt, which would entail a return to a life of idolatry and slavery. This book includes the story of Korah and his companions (Numbers 16:1-35) and the red heifer (Numbers 19:1-22), both of which have important parallels in the Qur'an (28:76-82 and 2:67-74, respectively). The book of Deuteronomy contains a second telling of the Law and a summary of the history of the Hebrew people up to the time of their arrival at Canaan. The book ends with the story of the death of Moses (Deuteronomy 34:1-12), in which God shows the Promised Land to Moses from across the Jordan River and tells him that he shall not enter it. Rather, God breathes life out of Moses and buries him where no one will find his grave.

Despite the fact that Moses figures prominently in the books of Exodus through Deuteronomy, he does not retain this prominence in the rest of Hebrew scripture or in Judaism. The simple reason for this is that Moses is not God, nor is he to be considered in any way divine (Kirsch 1998). Rather, Moses was a man like any other, and while he was selected by God to carry out an important historical task for the Hebrew people, Judaism is not about the reverence of outstanding individuals or the sanctification of their deeds. It is about the worship of God, and living life in accordance with God's law.

Moses in the New Testament

The Christian Bible is made up of the Old Testament and the New Testament, which contains the Gospels (Matthew, Mark, Luke and John), the Acts of the Apostles, a number of letters (epistles), and the book of Revelation (an apocalyptic work dealing with the Day of Judgment and the return of Jesus). Moses is mentioned about 60 times in the New Testament, with about one-third of these instances being found in the Gospels.

In Matthew (17:1-8) Jesus goes up a high mountain to pray and he is transfigured (his face shines like the sun), and Moses and Elijah appear to him and converse with him. In Mark (10:3), in response to a question from some Jewish scholars about divorce, Jesus responds by asking them what Moses commanded them to do. In Luke (16:31) the spirit of Abraham appears to a dead rich man who asks that a righteous man who has passed away be sent to his brothers who were still living in order that they might repent and be saved. Abraham responds that just as they have not listened to Moses and the prophets, they will not be persuaded by someone who rises from the dead either. In John (6:31-33), Jesus tells some Jews that it was not Moses who gave their ancestors bread from heaven when they were in the wilderness, but God. As these examples illustrate, the Gospels link Jesus to the prophets, criticize the Jews for not heeding the prophets, and reinforce the notion that the prophets are human rather than divine.

There are two New Testament references to Moses outside the Gospels that are worth looking at as a preparation for examining how Moses is dealt with in the Qur'an. The first of these is from the Acts of the Apostles, and the second is from the epistle to the Hebrews.

The Acts of the Apostles provides a history of the activities of the disciples of Jesus in the period immediately following the ascent of Jesus into heaven. Stephen, one of seven individuals appointed to look after the daily needs of the growing Christian community in Jerusalem, is accused by the Jews of speaking blasphemous words against Moses and God (Acts 6:11). In response to his accusers (Acts 7:1-53), Stephen recounts the story of how the Hebrews were under oppression in Egypt, how Moses was called by God to confront Pharaoh and bring the Law, and how in spite of all the signs and wonders that they witnessed, including their deliverance from Egypt, the Hebrew people still refused to obey God, choosing to persecute God's prophet instead. The Jews are so incensed by Stephen's words that they stone him to death. Among other things, this story illustrates the extremes that people will go to in their efforts to hide from the truth. They act as if eliminating the messenger will eliminate the message.

In the epistle to the Hebrews (3:1-6), Moses is referred to as a faithful servant who might be placed in charge of a household. By comparison, Jesus is to be viewed as greater than Moses in that he is like a son who, when placed over a household, is a direct reflection and inheritor of the position of the father and founder of the house. The intention here is clearly to inform the Jews that, while Moses might be among the greatest of men, Jesus is divine.

Moses in the Qur'an

Even though the name of Moses appears so many times in the Qur'an, it is interesting to note that his name does not appear at all in surahs 41 through 114. Remembering that the textual order of the Qur'an is virtually the reverse order in which the surahs were revealed, this suggests that the story of Moses only becomes important once the basic message of the Qur'an is known. There is a logical explanation for this. The early surahs tend to focus on the fundamental tenets of the Oneness of God and the Day of Judgment. By contrast, the content of the later surahs is much more complex and multi-faceted, often containing responses to both theoretical and practical questions about Islam, some of which are likely to have arisen through dialogue with Jews.

Based on my reading of the Qur'an, I think that an examination of surahs 26 (*The Poets*), 27 (*The Ants*) and 28 (*The Story*) as a continuous sequence provides a key to understanding not only the role of Moses in the Qur'an and the early development of Islam, but also how the Qur'an is related to the Law of Moses and how Islam is related to Judaism more generally.

There are a few striking structural clues which suggest that these three surahs should be treated together. First, surah 26 begins with the isolated letters *ta sin mim*, surah 27 with *ta sin*, and 28 with *ta sin mim*. This pattern of letters would appear to indicate not only that the three surahs are related but also that the overall structure is chiastic; that is, our focus is directed towards the middle. As with the three-part structure of surah 108 (see chapter 1), it might be logical to anticipate that surahs 26 and 28 contain parallel and yet contrasting content, while surah 27 outlines a condition or central message, important for understanding the overall intention of the sequence. This interpretation is reinforced by the content of the first verse of each of these surahs, which makes reference to scripture. Surahs 26 and 28 begin by indicating: "These are the verses of the Scripture that make things clear," and surah 27 begins with "These are the verses of the Qur'an – a scripture that makes things clear." I would suggest that the direct reference to the Qur'an at the start of the central surah (27) must be of some significance. Further, the amount of space devoted to discussing Moses and the particular elements of the story of Moses that are discussed in each surah help us to develop a broader appreciation of the thematic content and stylistic devices used in the sequence. What follows is a brief overview of each of the three surahs, in preparation for examining them as if they were one continuous passage.

The Poets (26)

This surah contains 227 verses and displays the following basic structure:

Prologue (1-2)
Introduction (3-9)
Moses (10-68)
Other prophets (69-191)
The Qur'an (192-209)
The jinn (210-227)

The short prologue consists of the isolated letters and a reference to scripture, while verses 3 through 9 serve as an introduction to the rest of the surah. Unlike the prologue, which links this surah to the surahs that follow as well as to the rest of the Qur'an, the introduction provides initial insight into the thematic content of the surah, drawing attention to the frustration and difficulty of the task of prophecy, referring to God as the "Lord of Mercy" and ending with the statement: "There truly is a sign in this, though most of them do not believe: your Lord alone is the Almighty, the Merciful." Among other things this statement establishes a sort of poetic refrain that will appear again at the end of each sub-section in which a particular prophet is discussed (verses 68, 104, 122, 140, 159, 175 and 191), and then again in the center of the final section (verse 217). The title "Lord of Mercy" signals to the reader that it is the imminent active God, who created and cares for humanity that is being referred to here. The primary theme of the surah appears to be the denial of God's revelation each time it is sent.

The first major section (verses 10 to 68) deals with Moses and his encounter with Pharaoh. Pharaoh is mentioned 74 times in the Qur'an, most often in association with Moses (Kassis 1988: 431-32). The two key themes in this section are the establishment of the identity of the "Lord of the Worlds" and the contrast between the pagan magic of the Egyptian sorcerers and the divinely granted magic of Moses. The "Lord of the Worlds" is not only the creator, but also the one who provides guidance through his messengers. The section ends with the delivery of the Hebrew people from Egypt and the destruction of Pharaoh's army. It is interesting to note that there is no mention at this

85

point of Moses having received either wisdom, or the law (scripture), from God.

The central section (verses 69 to 191) is divided into six sub-sections, each devoted to a different prophet: Abraham, Noah, Hud, Salih, Lot and Shuayb. The theme of each sub-section is basically the same, illustrating that God's prophets are often ridiculed, and that those who reject God's message will be punished. With the exception of the story of Abraham, each subsection contains a common statement: "I ask no reward of you, for my only reward is with the Lord of the Worlds" (verses 109, 126, 145, 164 and 180). This line not only serves as a sort of poetic or rhythmic reiteration of a central theme, it also serves to make the point that the prophets, probably in contrast to people's expectations, were not interested in material or Earthly gains. The fact that this line does not appear in the Abraham story draws attention to the point that Abraham had a one-on-one encounter with God, being put to the ultimate test of submission (the sacrifice of his own son). Abraham's mission was not to bring a message to a particular people, but rather to serve as the exemplar of the ultimate personal response to God. The Abraham story is also different in that it contains two references to the "Lord of the Worlds", both times in contrast to the idols worshipped by previous generations, the first (77) as a means of illustrating the uselessness of the idols, and the second (98) to show how the idolaters will backtrack and blame others when they are challenged about their beliefs on the Day of Judgment.

Another interesting aspect of this section is that three of these prophets are known from the Hebrew scripture, while the other three are associated with pre-Islamic Arabia. We might interpret this to suggest that the message contained in this surah, and by extension in the whole of the Qur'an, is meant equally for all people, Jews and non-Jews, Arabs and non-Arabs. This pairing of prophets carries over to include Moses and Muhammad.

Verses 192 through 209 address the fact that it was the "Lord of the Worlds" who sent down the Qur'an. In contrast to the events related in the previous section, Muhammad's message is for the Arabs, and the Qur'an has been sent down in their language so that they may understand it. However, the section also draws attention to the fact that even learned Jews recognized that the Prophet's message had come from the One God. This point serves to link the Qur'an to the Torah and Muhammad to Moses. The section ends with a reminder that people are not punished until they have been sent a messenger.

The final section (210-227) is divided into two components separated by a brief central sequence (217-220) that begins with "the Almighty, the Merciful" and ends with "the All Hearing, the All Knowing". Between these two pairs of divine attributes, we learn that God observes Muhammad in prayer and among the worshippers, thus reiterating the notions of transcendence and imminence with respect to God's relationship with the Prophet, and with people more generally. As was clear in the central verse of *The Opening*, people worship

God and God provides guidance to people. The first part of this section states that the jinn did not bring down the Qur'an, thus emphasizing not only the divine authorship of the message, but also the fact that people are likely to view the Qur'an as an act of sorcery. The second part deals again with the jinn, but shifts the emphasis to the poets and the people who follow them. This part illustrates the point that the jinn can in fact influence people through language, and have done so through some of the poets. The final verses appear to suggest that poetry is mere words that do not lead to action, whereas the words of the Qur'an lead to good deeds and the remembrance of God.

The Ants (27)

This surah, with 93 verses, is only slightly shorter than surah 26 and is structured as follows:

Prologue (1)
Introduction (2-6)
Moses (7-14)
Solomon (15-44)
Other prophets (45-58)
Theology (59-75)
Muhammad (76-93)

The prologue to this surah consists solely of the isolated letters. Verses 2 through 6, which might appear like a prologue are actually an introduction, which clearly demonstrates a chiastic structure, bracketed by direct references to the Qur'an and centering on the statement: "As for those who do not believe in the life to come, We have made their deeds seem alluring to them, so they wander blindly." The verses around this central message contrast the fates of the believers and the non-believers. The introduction ends with a reference to God as "One who is all wise and all knowing."

The story of Solomon (15-44) is bracketed by stories of the prophets. Verses 7 through 14 deal with Moses and verses 45 through 58 deal with Salih and Lot. In this version of the story of Moses we learn about his call to prophecy at the burning bush, which takes place prior to his encounters with Pharaoh. The Egyptians are destroyed for having enslaved the Hebrew people and for then refusing to heed God's message, as delivered by Moses, to let God's people go. Lot's people and the people of Thamud are destroyed for committing evil deeds.

In the Hebrew Bible (1 Kings 3:12), Solomon's great wisdom is attested to by God's words, saying: "I give you a heart so wise and understanding that there has never been anyone like you up to now, and after you there will come no one to equal you." In the Qur'an, Solomon demonstrates his wisdom first with respect to the ants and then in his treatment of the Queen of Sheba. The ants fear being crushed by Solomon and his vast armies, but Solomon smiles and thanks God for the blessings he has been granted. In a sense, Solomon is to the ants as God is to Solomon – so much greater in size and wisdom. Solomon sends a letter to the Queen of Sheba that begins with the *basmalah*, but she does not recognize it, as she and her people worship the sun. Sheba's throne is a symbol of her Earthly power and the theft of her throne in the blink of an eye, and her inability to positively identify it once it has been disguised, demonstrate the transitory and illusory nature of worldly goods and powers. When she is called into Solomon's great hall she believes that the mirrored floor is actually water. Being made aware of her mistake, she comes to the realization that she has been living in a false world, and she devotes herself to the "Lord of the Worlds."

Verses 59 through 75 address the two theological issues that are at the heart of the message of the Qur'an, namely, the Oneness of God and the Day of Judgment. These verses can be viewed as responding to an unasked question: "What is the content of the message that Solomon knew and shared with the Queen of Sheba, and that Moses and other prophets brought to various peoples, who stubbornly refused to listen?"

The final section deals specifically with Muhammad, especially in relationship to the message that he now brings and that has been brought before. Muhammad's identity and role are delineated in a series of declarations he is to make to the people. First, he is identified as the prophet for Makkah, as one who is devoted to God, and as someone who is only here to warn. Perhaps most significantly, he is instructed to say, "I am commanded to recite the Qur'an."

The Story (28)

This surah contains 88 verses and is structured basically as follows:

Prologue (1-2)
Moses (3-43)
Muhammad (44-75)
Qarun (76-82)
Conclusion (83-88)

As with surah 26, the prologue contains the isolated letters and a reference to scripture. At verse 3, the story of Moses begins with a reference to Pharaoh, but we are soon taken back to the childhood of Moses and the events that took place long before he was called to prophecy and to the task of bringing the Hebrews out of Egypt. Among other things we learn that God gave Moses knowledge and wisdom, that Moses sought mercy and forgiveness from God after killing a man, that Moses asked God for guidance, and that Moses spent ten years as a shepherd in Midian, where he got married, before responding to God's call.

One element of the Moses story that is unique to this surah is the story of Haman and the request from Pharaoh for Haman to bake bricks and build a tower, so that Pharaoh can climb up and see the God of Moses. Omar (2004: 598) indicates that Haman is not a proper name, but rather a reference to the role of Egyptian high priest. Thus, in a sense, Pharaoh is calling upon the representative of a pagan god to challenge the representative of the One God. There is a character known as Haman in the Hebrew Bible (Esther), who set out on a campaign to destroy all the Jews in the Persian Empire, but he was not Egyptian and he lived many centuries later than the events being related in the Qur'an. During their period of bondage, the Hebrew people were employed making bricks for Pharaoh, and the idea of the tower in reminiscent of the story of the Tower of Babel from the book of Genesis (11). In the Genesis story, God confounds the language of the people so that they are no longer able to communicate together effectively, thus bringing construction to a halt. While there is no direct explanation for the inclusion of this story in the Qur'an, it is interesting to note that the revelation of the Arabic Qur'an in a sense acts as a unifying element for the Arab people, using a common language to bring them closer to God through the book.

The next fairly lengthy section can be viewed as a direct effort to link Moses and Muhammad, as well as the Torah and the Qur'an (especially verse 49). The section draws together many of the lessons provided earlier in this surah and throughout the previous two surahs, placing them squarely in the context of emergent Islam. The surah even appears to come to a theological and structural conclusion with verse 70, with the affirmation of the Oneness of God and God's judgment, and the recognition that all praise belongs to Him. However, the next sequence of verses returns to a more conversational tone, further challenging those who do not believe the message, perhaps as a preparation for the Qarun story that follows.

Qarun is an arrogant individual who believes that the power and wealth he has accumulated are as a result of his own knowledge and efforts alone. As a punishment, God has the Earth open up and swallow Qarun and his household, providing a lesson to those who would deny the truth. The story is told in great detail in the book of Numbers (16:1-35), and perhaps its inclusion here is yet another attempt to demonstrate to the Jews the truth of the Qur'an, or perhaps it is an attempt to demonstrate to the Arabs the continuity from the Torah to the Qur'an, and from Moses to Muhammad.

The concluding section (83-88) appears to be a briefer version of verses 56 through 70, with a prefatory comment that links directly to the Qarun story. One outstanding feature of this final sequence is the statement in the final verse: "Everything will perish except His Face." Haleem (1999: 112) points out that this should not be interpreted as an effort to anthropomorphize God. Rather, it is an effective means of contrasting the limited vision, hearing and voice of humans with the eternal vision, hearing and voice of God.

Moses and Muhammad

Treating these three surahs as a continuous sequence in a sense mimics the learning process, whether oral or written. The first time we listen to a lecture, or read a page, we see or hear the message, but we are really engaged in a passive process, as if waiting for something to capture our attention. The second time, we are engaged in an active process of listening rather than merely hearing, allowing us to take in the message. The third time, we have an opportunity to reflect on the content and structure of the message, not only paying attention to the external signal, but in a sense following along in our own minds, ready to fill in gaps, increase understanding, and to some extent take ownership of the message. In the case of these three surahs, the structure and content of the message, as well as the style of delivery, becomes more complex and detailed as we work our way through what is basically the re-iteration of the same material. Variety is included to retain interest and help with comprehension, but when all is said and done, there is one lesson. Muhammad has been chosen to bring God's message to a hostile audience, and he is provided with the model of Moses to strengthen his resolve.

As mentioned earlier (chapter 2), the actual names of the surahs do not seem to have generated much interest among either the early commentators or modern scholars. However, the names that we have for these surahs do fit with the overall interpretation constructed here. *The Poets* is poetic and rhythmic in structure, with short verses and a great deal of repetition, thus aiding memory, and setting up an audible similarity with secular poetry, at the same time as presenting a contrast in content. The theme of magic plays an important role throughout this surah, contrasting God's magician (Moses) with Pharaoh's magicians, and contrasting God's inspiration of Muhammad with the jinn's inspiration of the poets. *The Ants* shifts the focus from magic to wisdom, and begins a process of drawing out the deeper content of the message, in terms of its theological underpinnings and its applicability to all people at all times. *The Story* is not just the story of Moses, but also the story of the hardship of prophecy and of the endless challenges that emerge to the authority of the prophets and ultimately to God's authority. It is interesting to observe that the details of the life of Moses go backward in time as we move through the surahs. In surah 26, the story of Moses starts with his encounters with Pharaoh. In surah 27, the timeline moves back to include the call to prophecy. Finally, in surah 28, we learn about Moses as an infant. Moses not only took God's message to the people, but through this biographical device we learn that Moses was very much an ordinary man, very much in need of God's guidance (28:22).

It might be too much of an oversimplification to suggest that there is one central message at the heart of these three surahs. However, given the importance of the *basmalah* within the context of the Qur'an as a whole, I think it is fair to suggest that there must be some very special reason to have it occur in the midst of a story about a wise man of God and his encounter with the ruler of a pagan kingdom. At one level, I think it is there to demonstrate that the Qur'an was delivered to a people who were caught between a pagan heritage and a monotheistic environment. On another level, and perhaps more in keeping with the broader intention of these three surahs, I think it serves to remind all people that as great as Moses was, and Muhammad was to become, they, like every other prophet, carried out their work, not in their own name, but in the name of God, the Lord of Mercy, the Giver of Mercy.

6

Prophets and Personalities
(Qur'an 31, 19:16-40, 18:83-102)

The previous two chapters dealt with individuals who are well known to Jews, Christians and Muslims, and to whom many verses in the Qur'an are devoted. Other personalities who are named in the Qur'an, such as Dhu l-Kifl and Haman, are mentioned only briefly, and in most instances these individuals cannot be linked with any certainty to particular historical figures. A few others, such as Luqman and Dhu l-Qarnayn, who are dealt with in this chapter, receive fairly limited coverage in the Qur'an, but their stories have become very well known among Muslims for reasons that will be explored below. As a starting point however, looking at the list of personalities who are named in the Qur'an, an interesting question emerges. Why are certain individuals identified by name, and not others? There are several possible answers.

First, the majority of those individuals who are named in the Qur'an are prophets whose stories can also be found in the Hebrew Bible and the New Testament, thus providing continuity for Islam with the earlier Abrahamic faiths. These would include such figures as Aaron, Abraham, Adam, Ezra, Job, John the Baptist, Jonah and Noah. Second, a number of other prophets, with whom Jews and Christians would not be familiar, also appear in the Qur'an. These would include Hud, Salih and Shuayb. Perhaps their stories are included as a means of demonstrating to the growing Islamic community that God has also operated in the world outside of Judaism and Christianity, having selected certain individuals, including some Arabs, in previous times and places to receive a message consistent with what is now being revealed to Muhammad. Third, important contemporary individuals (e.g., Abu Lahab), who would be known to the people of Makkah and Madina, are mentioned to provide local context and grounding for the Qur'an. Fourth, the names might serve as memory aids, providing a sort of convenient shorthand reference for some complex and yet critical notion (a literary device known as metonymy). For example, with respect to the first individual whose story is examined below, the mere mention of the name Luqman, once his story had been told, would stand in for having to recount the whole story at some point in the future.

Moving forward, it is important to remember that the number of verses in the Qur'an devoted to a particular theme or individual is not a measure of their significance. When reading the Qur'an we need to pay attention to both the content and the context of the various elements that we encounter. As mentioned earlier, commentators have generally treated the individual verses of the Qur'an as the basic unit of meaning and revelation. What should become clear in this chapter, and throughout this book more generally, is that a more comprehensive understanding of the Qur'an, and hence of Islam, will emerge when verses are examined in at least four distinct ways: the verses alone, the verses as part of an extended passage, all of the verses of a surah considered together, and the position and content of particular verses within the Qur'an as a whole (Mir 2004b).

Luqman (31:12-19)

Surah 31 (*Luqman*) contains 34 verses, and gets its name from the story of Luqman that is related in verses 12 through 19. While we are not going to carry out a thorough examination of the entire surah at this point, I have divided the verses into thematic segments in order to assist in the process of developing a more holistic understanding of the Luqman story, as suggested above.

Isolated letters (1) – see chapter 9
The Qur'an (2-5)
Distracting tales (6-9)
Creation (10-11)
Luqman (12-19)
Creation and the Qur'an (20-28)
The Day of Judgment (29-34)

The first major section (2-5) identifies the Qur'an (a "wise scripture") as a guide for the faithful, while the second section (6-9) warns against being led astray by "distracting tales". The third section (10-11) describes some aspects of God's creation and poses the challenge of demonstrating what other gods have created. Leaving aside the Luqman story for a moment, the fifth section (20-28) combines the themes of the first and third sections by addressing the creation of the Qur'an. It also speaks about those who ignore God's message, preferring to carry on the religious traditions of their ancestors. The final section (29-34) draws all of these themes together and looks ahead to the Day of Judgment, when all people will be called to account for their actions and beliefs. Turning now to the verses of the Luqman story, there are two possible versions of the structure:

    Luqman (12-19)
    or
    Luqman (12-13)
    Parents (14-15)
    Luqman (16-19)

It is not immediately clear when reading this passage in the Qur'an whether verses 12 through 19 actually form one continuous sequence. There are several possibilities. First, verses 12 through 19 might be part of the original surah, or they might be an interpolation. Similarly, verses 14 and 15 might be either part of the original surah or an interpolation within an interpolation, thus breaking the Luqman story into two distinct parts. It is even possible that the Luqman story (verses 12-13 plus verses 16-19) is an early interpolation, and that verses 14 and 15 represent a later interpolation into the previously interpolated Luqman story. Whatever the case might be, these alternatives raise an interesting methodological point.

In attempting to determine the structure and thematic content of a particular surah, it is sometimes useful to remove a sequence of verses that address a particular topic and appears to differ from the surrounding material. The objective in doing so is to see if the remaining verses still make sense. In other words, does the thematic or structural integrity of the surah appear to be intact, even without these verses? Similarly, if some verses are much longer than adjacent verses, or display a different grammatical structure or a shift in vocabulary, then removing them might aid in determining the overall thematic structure and content of the surah. It then becomes the task of the reader to explain the function of the removed verse or verses. So, as we observed when examining surahs 73 and 74 (see chapter 2), the surahs made complete sense when the respective interpolated long verses were removed. Upon further examination, it became clear that the added verses, in each case, served to further clarify thematic material that was already contained in the surahs.

In the case of surah 31, in verse 11, the Qur'an is speaking about God's creation and asks the disbelievers to demonstrate what the other gods have created. In verse 20, we return to the theme of the creator God and to the audacity of the disbelievers in suggesting that someone or

something other than God can create. From this observation, it is possible to conclude that the surah appears to
make complete sense with the story of Luqman removed.
At the same time, as a test of this conclusion, we might
look to see if the story of Luqman contributes in any way
to the theme of creation or to the overall message of the
surah, whatever that might be.

Following one possible interpretation of the structure, the story of Luqman is divided into three sections.
In the first section (12-13), not only is an individual
named, but we also read that this individual was given
wisdom. The concept of wisdom is used quite sparingly
(20 times) in the Qur'an (Kassis 1983: 525), and generally it is used in association with the concept of the
book (scripture). The importance of this connection will
become clearer as our analysis progresses. In these two
verses, Luqman is speaking to his son, telling him not to
attribute others to God. This instruction draws out the
two-sided nature of the concept of monotheism – not
only is there one God, but God is One.

In the second section (14-15), neither Luqman nor
his son is mentioned, and God is commanding all children to be good to their parents, especially their moth-
ers who carried them and fed them. They are told to
follow their parents in living life according to what is
right. At the same time however, children are instructed to disobey their parents, if their parents attempt to
get them to associate others with God; in other words,
if they are trying to get them to accept polytheism.

The third section (16-19) returns to Luqman, who tells
his son that nothing, no matter how small and insignificant

it may seem, escapes God's attention. He instructs his son to live a well-balanced life in accordance to what is right, and not to be arrogant. The section comes to a close with Luqman advising his son to go at a moderate pace with a lowered voice, remarking that the ugliest of voices is that of braying asses (perhaps a reference to the disbelievers and the tellers of distracting tales).

The two most obvious problems associated with treating this sequence of verses as a single unit, are the fact that Luqman and his son are absent from the central verses and the fact that the central verses are narrated by God and addressed to all people, thus constituting a shift in both narrator and audience. At the same time, the reference to not associating others with God appears in the first part of Luqman's story as well as in the central verses, and the reference to doing what is right is mentioned in the central verses and in the second part of the Luqman story.

Based on this analysis, we might suggest that verses 14 and 15 are part of the original surah and that the Luqman story was introduced to highlight the two central messages contained in these verses. By splitting the Luqman story into two pieces, a sort of chiastic or crossing structure is created with the outside or bracketing sections of the Luqman story pointing to the lessons in the central verses. Another interesting feature of this sequence of verses is that the Luqman story deals with a parent's obligation to teach a child, while the central section deals with the children's obligation to be good to their parents and heed their advice. Similarly, the Luqman story involves one individual addressing another, while the central verses involve God addressing all people. These contrasts help to accentuate both the structural and thematic focus of the verses.

Why this whole sequence is placed between verses 11 and 20 is less clear, as neither the story of Luqman, nor God's advice about parents appear to have anything to do with creation. However, in verse 11, the disbelievers are asked to present evidence of what the others (gods) have created, thus alluding to the theme of monotheism. More directly related to the Luqman story, the themes of doing right and following the example of parents, or forefathers, occur at various places in the surah, and there is one particular reference to parents and children that might in fact be the central message of the surah. In verse 33, the Qur'an cautions people that on the Day of Judgment no child can take the place of a parent and no parent can take the place of a child. Each individual will stand before God and be judged according to his or her own merits.

Perhaps the inclusion of verses 12 through 19 in this surah is meant to provide a build-up for verse 33, thus strengthening the message. There is no way for us to determine with accuracy or certainty if any aspect of this interpretation is actually the case. The objective of performing the type of analysis we have just gone through here is to help us dig deeper into the text, so that we can increase our overall understanding of the message of the Qur'an.

Finally, we might wonder why Luqman's name is mentioned in the Qur'an and why he has a surah named after him. According to Omar (2004: 515), Luqman, a Nubian, who was neither a Jew nor an Arab, lived in the time of David (ca. 1000 BCE) and was the subject of a celebrated poem written in the sixth century CE by Nabigha al-Dhubyani. According to tradition, Luqman is viewed as a model of wisdom, spiritual maturity, and of how a person should live. His story certainly would have been familiar to the Arabs at the time of the Prophet. However, unlike Moses, Jesus and Muhammad, Luqman receives wisdom, but no book. In spite of this fact, Luqman passes wisdom on to his own child, just as this surah passes wisdom on to all children. The second verse contains the phrase "wise scripture." Even without a scripture, Luqman is able to pass wisdom to his son. Notwithstanding the advice and important role of parents, the wise child is the one who learns wisdom from the Qur'an.

Mary and Jesus (19:16-40)

The story of Mary in the Qur'an is quite remarkable for several reasons. Not only does Mary get a surah named after her, but she is also the only woman to be referred to by name in the Qur'an (Stowasser 1994: 67). Furthermore, she is not only the mother of Jesus, but she is actually mentioned more often than Jesus throughout the Qur'an, as a model of chastity and modesty, in a sense the ideal female servant of God. In this respect, the Islamic reverence for Mary follows the example set by Jesus, who remarks (19:32) that God has commanded him to cherish his mother.

The story of Mary also allows us to gain insight into a controversial issue surrounding the authorship of the Qur'an and its relationship to the scripture of the Jews and Christians. In verse 28 when Mary appears to her people with the infant Jesus, they say to her: "Sister of Aaron!" Critics of the Qur'an have pointed to this incident as a demonstration that the Qur'an is merely a compilation of fragments from prior scripture, with some additional Arab material thrown in to give it local context (Wansbrough 1977). Their reasoning for this is based on the fact that there was a Mary (Miriam in Hebrew) who was the sister of Aaron and Moses, and in referring to the mother of Jesus as the sister of Aaron, the authors of the Qur'an are demonstrating not only their ignorance of Hebrew scripture, but also their ignorance of time scales and family relationships. Defenders of the Qur'an and its divine authorship have countered this argument with the interpretation that in referring to Mary as a sister of Aaron, the people are highlighting her paternity in the tribe of Levi and the lineage of Aaron, rather than actually suggesting that Mary was literally Aaron's sister (Yusuf Ali 2004: 750). From my perspective, both of these positions appear overly simplistic, distracting us from the larger theological and practical significance of the reference.

Perhaps the key to understanding the deeper meaning of this reference is to recognize that the phrase 'sister of Aaron' is being hurled at Mary like an accusation. It is not just a passing reference, or a clarification, as if to separate her from other girls named Mary. Instead, this accusation would serve as a reminder to the Jews, and to Mary, of events that took place in the wilderness when Moses was struggling to get the Hebrew people to the Promised Land. In the book of Numbers (12:1-

16), Aaron and Miriam complain about the leadership of Moses, grumbling about their own positions with respect to carrying out God's work. God punishes Miriam by afflicting her with leprosy, but Aaron and Moses intervene on her behalf and God immediately returns her to good health. However, God points out that in accordance with His law one who has brought shame to the community is to be cast out of the camp for seven days. Thus, Miriam spends a week separated from her people and the sojourn of the Hebrew people only continues upon her return. The parallel to Mary's actions, as related in the Qur'an, is obvious. She has separated herself from the community and upon her return she is carrying a child in her arms, demonstrating in a sense the basis for her shame and separation. The accusation from her people serves to communicate the sentiment that Mary has truly lived up to the actions and example of her namesake. I would suggest that this deeper interpretation, based on familiarity with the book of Numbers, would not be lost on the Arabs as they heard Mary's story in the Qur'an.

Other events from the book of Numbers figure prominently in the Qur'an, especially the story of Qarun in surah 28, as discussed in the previous chapter, and the story of the unblemished cow in surah 2 (see chapter 9). The use of these two stories along with the story of Mary suggests two important points. First, it seems likely that the Arabs were quite familiar with the scripture of the Jews. Second, the book of Numbers appears to have had special significance with respect to the way that God's message was revealed to Muhammad. The book of Numbers deals primarily with the forty-year struggle that Moses faced in trying to get the Hebrew people to accept God and to follow God's law. In the early phase of the establishment of Islam, Muhammad's interactions with the Arabs strongly parallel those of Moses with the Hebrew people during their time in the wilderness.

Returning to Mary, when her people chastise her for having a child out of wedlock, it is the baby Jesus who responds. He indicates that he is a servant of God and that God has granted him the scripture. From his comments we might get the impression that the infant Jesus in some sense incorporates the scripture, as demonstrated partially by his ability to speak and by the content of what he says. This interpretation would be consistent with the image of Jesus presented in the Gospel of John, where Jesus is equated with the Word of God – Jesus is the Word. From this perspective then, it is plausible to suggest that when the Qur'an refers to the Gospel, it is not referring to the four literal Gospels of the New Testament, but rather to the person Jesus. By extension, and perhaps as an explanation of why Mary is the only woman named in the Qur'an, Mary can be viewed as the one who brought the message (Jesus) to her people (Stowasser 1994: 76-77).

Dhu l-Qarnayn (18:83–102)

In surah 18 (*The Cave*), verses 83 through 102, we find the story of Dhu l-Qarnayn. Like Luqman, the story of this individual is unique to the Qur'an, appearing in neither the Torah nor the Gospels. It is also noteworthy from the point of view that, in contrast to the more localized orientation of the rest of the Qur'an (Makkah and Madina), it refers to distant travels and encounters with other peoples (i.e., non-Semites). As with Luqman, our primary goal in studying this passage is to determine why his story is told in the Qur'an, and why it is told in this specific location in the Qur'an. In contrast to the story of Luqman, the story of Dhu l-Qarnayn has fuelled a great deal of speculation as to the historical identity of this figure.

The most common opinion among scholars, Muslim and non-Muslim, is that Dhu l-Qarnayn is Alexander the Great (Renard 2001: 61-62; Stoneman 2008; Yusuf Ali 2004: 738-42). The primary justification for this attribution is the fact that the details of the account of Dhu l-Qarnayn's travels, as presented in the Qur'an, can be matched quite readily with particular historical and geographic correlates. For example, the description of the western limit of his travels as bringing him to a place where the sun appeared to set into a muddy spring has been linked to a location in ancient Illyricum (near the present border of Albania and Croatia), where water emerges from an underground spring in the mountains, discolored because of its high mineral content. This location formed a natural defense to the west of Alexander's home in Macedon. Similarly, Alexander goes east and builds a wall in a mountain pass to protect a people who could barely understand him from invaders. The location of this wall has been identified as being southeast of Bukhara on the route from Turkestan to India. We learn from the accounts of a seventh century Chinese traveler, Hiouen Tsiang, and from the record of an expedition to this location sponsored by the ninth century Abbasid caliph al-Wathiq, that remnants of the wall in accordance with the description given in the Qur'an could still be identified. A lake in close proximity to the mountain pass is known as Iskander Kul (in modern Tajikistan). Finally, the name Dhu l-Qarnayn translates to "the two-horned one" (Omar 2003: 453). From historical documents and depictions on coins, we know that Alexander sometimes referred to himself as an incarnation or representative of the god Jupiter, who is often shown with horns on his head, representing his association with the bull, a symbol of strength and of masculine potency. Also, the idea of the two horns might be interpreted as representing East and West, or the geographical extremes of Alexander's conquests.

Why would the Qur'an mention a Greek conqueror that lived 900 years prior to the time of the revelation? One explanation for this is that Alexander can be viewed as a unifier and thus an example to be followed by Muhammad (Yusuf Ali 2004: 731). From the specific locations mentioned in the Qur'an, and from the actions taken by Dhu l-Qarnayn, we see that more often than not, he did not fight. Rather, he attempted to bring people into a more unified and peaceful kingdom, passing on culture, language and security. The Greek language and Hellenistic culture served for centuries as a common basis for everything from commerce to intellectual pursuits in an area that extended from Greece to India and south to Egypt (Ostler 2005: 227-71). Similarly, Arabic, through the medium of the Qur'an, was intended to unify the known world through the message of the One God that it conveyed (Ostler 2005: 93-112).

As with the story of Luqman, if we remove the story of Dhu l-Qarnayn from surah 18, we can assess to what extent the story appears to be an interpolation. In verses 60 to 82, there is a parable about Moses traveling to the place where the two seas meet that involves an encounter with a curious stranger. As mentioned earlier (see chapter 2), a parable is a story composed of familiar elements that is used to convey a moral or religious message. In this particular story God protects the property of two orphans who would have otherwise lost their inheritance due to the misdeeds of others. The section beginning at verse 103 deals with the question of who has the most to lose by their misguided actions, even when they believe they are doing something good. At first glance then it appears that the story of Dhu l-Qarnayn is an interpolation, breaking up what would otherwise be a logical sequence in the text. However, as Yusuf Ali (2004: 738-40) suggests, even if there is some historical correlate for the story of Dhu l-Qarnayn, its likely purpose at this juncture in the Qur'an is to serve as a parable, just like the story of Moses in the preceding verses.

David and the Psalms

As a means of drawing this chapter to a close, I want to discuss some of the references in the Qur'an to other scripture, especially the Psalms. So far, we have

seen numerous references to events related in the Torah, especially from the book of Numbers, and the
Qur'an confirms that a book was given to Moses as a
guide and mercy to the people (46:12). Similarly, the
Qur'an acknowledges the revelation of the Gospel of
Jesus (3:3, 3:48), which contained guidance and light,
and a confirmation of the law given to Moses (5:46).
In the Qur'an, the well-known biblical figure David is
mentioned as the slayer of Goliath (2:251), as a maker of chain mail armor, God having softened iron for
him (34:10-11), and as the receiver of a book (17:55).
David's place among the prophets and the apparently
special significance of the book given to him are high-
lighted in the following verse:

> *We have sent revelation to you [Prophet] as We did to*
> *Noah and the prophets after him, to Abraham, Ishmael,*
> *Isaac, Jacob, and the Tribes, to Jesus, Job, Jonah, Aaron,*
> *and Solomon — to David We gave the book [of Psalms] — to*
> *other messengers We have already mentioned to you, and*
> *also to some We have not. (4:163)*

Among other things, this verse highlights the notion
of the continuity of prophecy through the ages, and
the linkage through revelation of Jews, Christians and
Muslims. It is not clear from this verse alone why the
Psalms are singled out for direct mention, but it does
serve to place David's book on a level shared with the
Qur'an, the Torah and the Gospel.

The Psalms do stand out however, when compared

to the other scriptures revealed prior to the Qur'an, in that it is the only scripture that is cited in a direct manner in the Qur'an. In surah 21 (*The Prophets*), we read:

We wrote in the Psalms, as We did in [earlier] Scripture:
"My righteous servants will inherit the earth."
(21:105)

This statement appears in slightly different forms in three places in the Psalms (25:13, 37:11, 37:29) and, as suggested in this verse, a similar statement can be found in Exodus (32:13). Furthermore, the statement appears again in the words of Jesus, as recorded in the gospel of Matthew (5:5), thus providing an explicit link between the scriptures revealed to Moses, David, Jesus and Muhammad.

As a final note, the Qur'an states that a book was also revealed to Abraham (53:37, 87:19), but no such book has come down to us.

7

The Day of Judgment
(Qur'ān 99, 81, 82, 101, 50)

Eschatology

Unlike the previous few chapters that have focused on individuals, this chapter and the next are primarily thematic in content, focusing on the warning of an impending day of judgment that comprises the central message of the majority of the early short surahs. The concept of a day of judgment is one component of what is referred to as an eschatology – an explanation of the end times. Not only does a particular eschatology commonly contain the theme of judgment, it also often makes reference to a catastrophic event, known as an apocalypse, which will signal the arrival of the period of judgment, or otherwise bring an end to the world as we know it. While absent from the Torah, apocalyptic themes are common in the prophetic books of the Jews, especially the books of Daniel and Isaiah.

> *The earth will burst asunder, the earth will be shaken apart, the earth will be convulsed. The earth will reel like a drunkard, and it will slay like a hut. Its rebellion will weigh it down, until it falls, never to rise again.* (Isaiah 24:19-20)

By comparison, the notion of a day of judgment is less explicit in Jewish scripture, but becomes a major theme of Christian scripture and doctrine, with a focus on the return of Jesus, as documented particularly in the New Testament book of Revelation.

> *I saw the dead, the great and the lowly, standing before the throne, and scrolls were opened. Then another scroll was opened, the book of life. The dead were judged according to their deeds, by what was written in the scrolls.* (Revelation 20:12)

Eschatology is a major theme of the message presented in the Qur'an and it remains so in the later development of Islamic theology (see Cook, 2002, 2005).

The Earthquake (99)

This short surah contains one of the most concise and evocative statements in the Qur'an of what will take place on the Day of Judgment. At the same time, this surah also provides an excellent demonstration of four common literary devices used throughout the Qur'an, especially when issues related to eschatology are being discussed. The first such device is the repeated use of the word "when" to introduce signs of the coming judgment. The repetition of this conditional word builds a sense of anticipation in the reader and helps to emphasize the fact that we do not know when "when" is. The second device is the use of signs to describe the anticipated events. These signs tend to be apocalyptic (an earthquake in this instance), presenting a stark contrast to the natural order of things as represented by the systematic passage of time through the seasons, and a person's usual life course. The third device is what might be referred to as a mercantile reference, drawing upon the knowledge of business and trade that the Makkan Arabs would possess. For example, the idea of being weighed and being held to account provides a familiar metaphor, or business analogy, for a future judgment that will involve measuring the amount of good and evil that a person has engaged in throughout their lifetime. The fourth device encompasses the use of scientific or cosmological metaphors. At one end of the scale we have a cataclysmic event such as the shaking of the earth, that is unpredictable, both in terms of when it will happen and what its exact consequences will be. At the other end of the scale we are presented with the notion of an atom's weight – something that many people might consider as insignificant and inconsequential. The use of the idea of the weight of an atom should not be interpreted to suggest that somehow the Qur'an contains knowledge of the physical composition of matter that physicists would only articulate in the early 1900s. Rather this term is simply a modern substitute for the Arabic word that was used to indicate the weight of an ant or a grain of sand; in other words, something so small that it could not be divided any further.

Surah 99 also contains a reminder that people are the focus of God's creation and of the Day of Judgment. One of the signs alluded to here is that of the earth throwing out its burdens. As this sign immediately precedes the judgment scene, one logical interpretation of this sign is to equate people in their graves with the burden being cast out. People, both good and bad, have been stored in the ground awaiting judgment and thus the quaking serves to thrust these people into the moment of judgment while at the same time returning the earth to its pristine created form.

Shrouded in Darkness (81)

Surah 81 is about three times the length of surah 99, and thematically it can be divided into three sections. In the first section (1-14), a number of apocalyptic signs are described and a sense of urgency is created through the repeated use of the word 'when' at the beginning of each short verse. This mechanism gives the surah a hurried and breathless quality that serves to underscore the seriousness of the message as well as the element of surprise. No one knows when the Day of Judgment will come and many will be caught unprepared. As Yusuf Ali (2004: 1606) points out, there are twelve signs mentioned in these verses, divided into two groups of six. The first six deal with physical aspects of life, while the last six deal with inner or spiritual existence. Among the signs are fantastical images such as the seas boiling over, the mountains being put in motion and the wild beasts being herded together. Apocalyptic images like these are also common in the scripture of the Jews and Christians, for example, in the prophetic book of Isaiah (65:25), where we read: "The wolf and the lamb shall graze alike, and the lion shall eat hay like the ox." Also, within both groups of signs, there are direct appeals to the life experience of the Arabs. For example, the idea of abandoning a pregnant camel would be shocking to the Arabs, as camels were an essential component of economic wellbeing. Similarly, the idea that baby girls would rise from their graves to question the actions of their parents serves as a strong indictment of the common pagan Arab practice of female infanticide.

In the middle section (15-25), God is addressing the people in the form of an oath, invoking all of creation in support of Gabriel and, by extension, Muhammad (Yusuf Ali 2004: 1609). This sequence of verses provides a good illustration of the difficulty that emerges at times when reading the Qur'an, with respect to keeping the identity of individuals straight as they are being referred to by personal pronouns, rather than directly by name. In verse 19, the noble messenger referred to is the angel Gabriel, and the following passages indicate that he is held in high esteem in the heavens. The companion mentioned in verse 22 is Muhammad, and in verse 23 when it says, "he did see him," it means that Muhammad did see Gabriel. In verse 24, the pronouns "He" and "him," both refer to Muhammad. The meaning of the section as a whole is that both Muhammad and the intermediary Gabriel are carrying out God's will and that they are not coming under the influence of an evil spirit. The substance of the oath is to make clear that all of God's creation is witness to this fact.

The final section (26-29) of this surah has a somewhat rhetorical ring to it as it asks the people where they
are going. In other words, it appears to be saying "Now
that you have heard the message of the Qur'an, why are
you not following the straight path – the path that God
has provided for you?" People can choose not to follow
the straight path, but the consequences of this choice are
clear. If, instead, people choose to do as God has willed
for them, then they will be rewarded accordingly.

Torn Apart (82)

The opening verses of this surah parallel those of surah
81 in structure and content, lending support to the
view of some commentators (e.g., Islahi) that many of
the surahs in the Qur'an form natural pairs that are
meant to be recited together to aid memory and understanding (Robinson 2003: 272). Certainly the strong
parallels that we observed when examining surahs 73
and 74 (see chapter 2) would support such a theory,
and in the next chapter I will explore to what extent
surahs 55 and 56 can be viewed in this way. However,
when comparing surahs 81 and 82, once you move past
the opening verses, the parallels do not appear to be
very strong. Surah 82 is much shorter than surah 81,
and its content does not divide up easily into three distinct thematic sections. Also, there are no direct references to either the Qur'an or Muhammad in surah
82. Finally, surah 82 makes use of two literary devices
not found in surah 81 that have parallels in surahs far
removed from this location in the Qur'an.

First, verses 11 and 12 make mention of "noble recorders" who keep track of people's actions. While the

"records of deeds" are referred to in verse 10 of surah 81, as they are in several other places in the Qur'an (e.g., 18:49, 54:52), the identification of individuals charged with the task of monitoring human action is much less common, being explored to the greatest extent, as we will see below, in surah 50. Second, the term "Day of Judgment" appears three times in close proximity, in verses 15, 17 and 18 of surah 82. The first occurrence of the term is in the form of a statement and the second and third occurrences are in the form of a question. This formula is also used in surah 101, verses 1 through 3, with the term "crashing blow" and in surah 69, verses 1 through 3, with the term "inevitable hour." The placement and phrasing of the formula in surahs 101 and 69 is exactly the same, with the occurrence in surah 82 showing some variation in both respects. Notwithstanding these differences, I think the effect of using the device is the same in each case. By repeating these eschatological terms in such close proximity, the importance and inevitability of the Day of Judgment would be reinforced to the reader (hearer).

The Crashing Blow (101)

As was the case with surah 82, this surah uses the three-fold iteration of a single term to emphasize its message. In this case, as just explained above, the term 'crashing blow' is found in each of the first three verses. This crashing blow will scatter people like moths and will scatter mountains like tufts of wool. The thematic content of this short surah is rather straightforward and to the point, beginning with an apocalyptic image, moving to judgment, and finishing with resurrection, either to a pleasant life or to the blazing fire of the bottomless pit. As with surah 99, judgment is depicted using a mercantile analogy, contrasting people whose good deeds weigh heavy on the scale with those whose good deeds are light. As will become clear in the next chapter, and in the examination of surah 50 below, this thematic structure of apocalypse, judgment, and resurrection is very common throughout the Qur'an.

Qaf (50)

Surah 50 is from a later period than the other surahs discussed in this chapter so far, and even though the thematic pattern of apocalypse, judgment, and resurrection outlined above is present in this surah, the discussion is somewhat more sophisticated theologically than is the case in the early surahs. For one thing there are two additional thematic elements, the Qur'an and creation, and the use of contrast and comparison is much more extensive.

Structurally, the surah is also rather elaborate, being laid out in the form of an extended chiasm. In other words, the thematic elements are laid out in a particular order from the opening verse towards the middle of the surah, and then the themes are repeated in reverse order from the middle of the surah towards the last verse. As Dorsey (1999) explains, there are several advantages to using chiasms:

1. Beauty: humans appreciate the esthetic quality of a balanced presentation.
2. Coherence: a symmetry's tight configuration reinforces its unity.

3. Sense of completeness: the audience can recognize when the composition is winding down, and they know it has concluded when it echoes its beginning. A symmetrically arranged piece comes full circle, ending where it began.

4. Central pivot: in a more extensive symmetry with an uneven number of units (e.g., A-B-C-D-C'-B'-A'), the central unit is the natural location for the turning point, climax, high point, or centerpiece, since it marks the point where the composition reverses its order. Both halves of the symmetry look toward the center unit, making it the natural focal point.

5. Memory aid: both speaker and audience can remember the successive point of a speech more easily with the aid of symmetric organization.

6. Opportunities to exploit the repetitions: as with the parallel pattern, repetitions provide opportunity to do such things as compare, contrast, reiterate, emphasize, explain, and illustrate. (31)

Many of these elements were illustrated well in *The Opening* (see chapter 3). However, I would not suggest that because of this the chiastic form should somehow be viewed as the ideal form for a surah, nor am I suggesting that all surahs follow this form. Rather, I am suggesting that, to the extent that this sort of analysis helps us to understand the message of the Qur'an, then, following the example of scholars who have uncovered chiasms in works as diverse as the books of the Torah and Homer's *Iliad*, we should be open to exploring this apparently powerful analytical tool.

Based on my reading of surah 50, I have identified the following chiastic structure:

A – Qur'an (1)
  B – what the disbelievers say (2)
   C – resurrection (3)
    D – disbelief (4-5)
     E – creation (6-11)
      F – disbelieving peoples (12-14)
       G – second creation (15)
        H – jugular vein – two receptors (16-18)
         I – truth and escape (19)
          J – trumpet and warning (20)
           K – two attendants (21-22)
            L – recorded evidence (23)
             M – hurl (24)
              N – hindered good, aggressive,
                 caused doubt, set up other gods
                 (25-26)
             M' – hurl (26)
            L' – transgression (27)
           K' – two attendants argue (28)
          J' – warning (28-29)
         I' – hell and paradise (30-31)
        H' – human actions – heart (32-33)
       G' – second creation (34-35)
      F' – disbelieving peoples (36-37)
     E' – creation (38)
          First aside to Muhammad (39-41)
    D' – disbelief (41-43)
   C' – resurrection (44)
  B' – what the disbelievers say (45)
      Second aside to Muhammad (45)
A' – Qur'an (45)

Prior to explaining some of the details of this structure, it is necessary to draw attention to a number of technical points. First, the pivotal verse in a chiasm does not necessarily need to be at the literal center of the surah, either with respect to verse number (in this case, the literal center verse would be 23), or with respect to the number of words on either side of the center (in this case, there are somewhat more words following the central verse). Furthermore, any given verse can contain several thematic elements that may constitute different components of the chiasm. For example, the first part of verse 28 has God instructing the two recorders not to argue in His presence (K'), while the second part of the verse refers to the fact that God had sent a warning (J'). Similarly, the amount of text devoted to individual elements does not have to match on both sides of the chiasm. For example, in the first half of the surah the topic of creation is covered in verses 6 through 11, while in the second half it is discussed in just one verse (38). Finally, there can be breaks in the symmetry of the chiasm, as in the case of the two asides directed to Muhammad that I have identified here. The fact that these elements break the symmetry serves to give particular emphasis to these verses, while at the same time serving to reinforce just how strong of an influence on the reader the chiastic structure can have.

Based on this analysis, the central theme of the surah (N), found in verse 25 and the first portion of verse 26, is that those who hindered good, were aggressive, caused others to doubt, and who set up other gods alongside God, will be sent to hell once they have been judged. Verses 24 and 26 (M-M'), surrounding the central message, both mention hurling the disbelievers into hell. The verb 'to hurl' in both instances is used in the dual. The use of the dual is particularly important here and in the next chapter, so it is worth spending some time trying to understand what it means, especially as this is one linguistic aspect of the Qur'an that can be lost in translation.

Grammatically, we are most accustomed to verbs being used either in the singular or the plural, with respect to number, and in first (I, we), second (you), or third (he/she/it, they), with respect to person. The ancient Semitic languages, as well as Classical Greek, along with now outdated forms of most Slavic languages make use of a form between the singular and plural, known as the dual. This verb form is used to signify action taken by two subjects that share a common characteristic. For example, two brothers, or a husband and wife, can be referred to in the dual, almost as if they are acting as one. In the next chapter when we examine surah 55, we will see that humans and jinns are referred to in the dual, as both are God's creatures. English has no dual, and so when translating this verb form, the word "both" is usually inserted to convey the proper meaning. In this case, the instruction "Hurl every obstinate disbeliever into Hell," in verse 24, should be interpreted as "[Both of you] hurl every obstinate disbeliever into Hell." Clearly from context the dual in this instance is referring to the two companions, one to drive the person on and the other to bear witness to the person's deeds.

The pairing between the content of the opening verses (A through G) and that of the final verses (G' through A') is based for the most part on direct word matches and clearly this pattern would aid in memorization as well as assist in bringing closure to the surah. Thematically, these verses draw attention to three ideas that the Arabs had great difficulty in believing about the revelation that was being presented to them by the Prophet. First, they had difficulty with the form of the message, namely, the Qur'an. Second, they had trouble believing that Muhammad could be the deliverer of the message. Finally, they could not accept the notion that there would be life after death.

The links between some of the other pairs are based on various complementary and contrasting images that help to provide a more thorough understanding of the concepts being described. For example, by linking the jugular vein to the heart (H-H') in conjunction with the words whisper and devotion, attention can be drawn to the way in which the physical aspect of human existence and the life of the soul are intertwined. Similarly, in another pairing (I-I'), truth is linked with paradise and hell is linked with "what you tried to escape." As a final example (L-L'), a reference to the recorded evidence of a person's deeds is linked to the fact that the companion did not have to entice the person to transgress, as "he had already gone far astray by himself."

I have identified two asides directed at Muhammad, which appear to break the symmetry of the chiasm. The first one, in verses 39 through 41, instructs Muhammad to be patient, to celebrate and proclaim the praise of God, and to listen out for the Day of Judgment. The placement of this aside just before the return of the theme of the disbelievers serves to establish a contrast between Muhammad and those who will not heed the message, while at the same time providing instructions and an example for those who will heed the message. The second aside is in the middle of final verse (45), where God points out to Muhammad that he cannot force people to believe, he can only remind them with the Qur'an. In a sense this aside serves as a brief reiteration of the first aside, while also emphasizing that the onus of belief is on the people and not on Muhammad. These direct comments to the Prophet demonstrate the reflexive quality of the Qur'an, in that Muhammad is the recipient of God's message in two distinct, but complementary, ways. First, with respect to this entire surah, for example, the Prophet receives the message and passes it on to those who will hear it. All hearers, including Muhammad, as receiver and transmitter, learn the content of the message. With respect to the asides directed at Muhammad, all listeners hear these words, but Muhammad is the recipient of these portions of the message in a way that other hearers are not, even though they also hear the content of these asides.

Clearly, there is much more that could be said about this surah and about the approach I have used for analyzing its contents. However, at this point, I want to emphasize again that I am not trying to impose my interpretation on the text of the Qur'an or on the reader. Rather, I am trying to expand the repertoire of analytical tools that readers can have at their disposal as they attempt to read and understand the Qur'an. By way of bringing this chapter to a close, I want to introduce a philosophical matter related to the notions of death and resurrection that have been raised in the surahs we have just examined.

Barzakh

The notion of *barzakh*, or partition, has particular significance for the development of Islamic metaphysics, as illustrated in the philosophical writings of Ibn Arabi (d. 1240 CE) and in the works of the illuminationists (Nasr 2006), especially Mulla Sadra (d. 1640 CE). The term appears just three times in the Qur'an (23:100, 25:53, 55:20) and in the latter two instances it is used to refer to the invisible division between fresh and salt water. In the third instance (23:100), the term refers to the state that people occupy between the time of their death and the moment of their resurrection (Haleem 1999: 87-88). As Omar (2004: 49) suggests, this is a state in which our concepts of space and time are meaningless. It is a state that we cannot conceive of, and yet according to a *hadith* recorded by Bukhari (Vol. 2, Bk. 23, No. 461), the Prophet stated: "When a person dies his abode in the Hereafter is brought before him morning and evening in Paradise, if he is one of the inmates of Paradise, and of Fire if he is one of the inmates of Hell." This tradition might be interpreted to suggest that immediately after a person's death, that individual soul is already aware of the final judgment that will be passed on it when the Day of Judgment comes. While the term *barzakh* is not used in this *ha-*

dith, the contents of the *hadith* are clearly referring to events that take place in this intermediary phase of human existence.

Chittick (1989) quotes Ibn Arabi as stating that *barzakh* is "something that separates a known from an unknown, an existent from a nonexistent, a negated from an affirmed, an intelligible from a non-intelligible" (118). From this definition we might assume that following a person's death, the individual passes into a realm of unknowing, a truly intermediary and indescribable state. In contrast, for Mulla Sadra, *barzakh* is the soul (Dakake 2004). According to this view, *barzakh* is not a partition, but rather the essential continuous element that joins this life with the next, present in all three modes of human existence, and in a sense actually constituting the intermediary mode of existence. This latter interpretation might be viewed as more consistent with the message contained in the *hadith*, but there is no way of determining with certainty whether the *hadith* should be taken literally, or as metaphor.

My immediate purpose in raising this issue is to draw attention to the way in which Islamic thought has responded to questions about what happens between the time of a person's death and the arrival of the Day of Judgment. Given the strongly eschatological tone of the Qur'an, it is natural to assume that this would have been a frequent question on the minds of those hearing the revelation.

Further, as with my brief overview of the "Light verse" (24:35) in chapter 3, I want to demonstrate that the task of understanding the Qur'an goes well beyond an examination of the obvious literal text, as given. Just as there is an essential metaphysical and mystical content to the Qur'an that only becomes evident through the recitation of the text in Arabic, there is a similarly esoteric layer of understanding of the Qur'an that can only be gleaned through systematically reading and analyzing the text. Whether this latter process can only be carried out through an exploration of the Arabic text of the Qur'an is an open question.

8

The Dual, Dualism and Pairing
(Qur'an 55, 56)

This chapter continues with the theme of eschatology, providing further illustrations of some of the concepts discussed in the previous chapter, such as the use of the dual, the idea that surahs appear in natural pairs, and the identification and significance of chiastic structure. At the same time, as reflected both in the title of this chapter and in the fact that our analysis will focus on two surahs (55 and 56) the discussion will be dominated by the number two and by various conceptions of "two-ness." Throughout the previous chapters, examples of complementary and contrasting pairs of concepts used to emphasize a particular point of interest have been illustrated, and as we will see below especially in surah 55 the Qur'an makes use of this device to its fullest. Looking more generally at the use of numbers as a literary device, I finish the chapter with a brief discussion of numerology in the Qur'an.

Diptych

The word diptych is Greek in origin and basically implies the notion of being folded in two. The most familiar use of this term is probably with respect to paintings that are rendered on two panels hung side by side. However, there is a long history of using portable diptychs as a means of transporting written communications. For this purpose, think of a diptych as the precursor of a binder, such as a student would use for holding notepaper. The diptych (binder) would be constructed out of a durable and rigid material (e.g., metal, wood, ivory), and it would be used to transport and protect documents that were written on single pages rather than on scrolls. Often diptychs were ornately decorated, and would sometimes contain a permanent message of their own, such as a passage from scripture or a royal decree.

In literary analysis it is common practice to use the term diptych to designate a written work made up of two parts. In this sense, the concept has been used extensively in analyses of the Torah (Brodie 2001) and the Qur'an (Robinson 2003), especially when discussing adjacent verses that contain similar content or illustrate parallel grammatical structure. In this chapter, I am using the idea of a diptych to express a particular kind of relationship that I think exists between surahs

55 and 56, but prior to outlining the details of that relationship I want to review some characteristics of chiastic structure.

The term chiasm is used to describe the structure of a document in which the statement of a particular series of textual components is followed by a repetition of those components in reverse order. Chiasms often have an uneven number of elements (e.g., A-B-C-B'-A'), as was the case with surah 50, pointing towards a central or core message. However, chiasms can also have an even number of elements (e.g., A-B-C-C'-B'-A') providing a literal reversal of parts or mirror image with no central thematic element. In these instances, repetition alone serves as a means of emphasis, with the reversal of order helping to remind the reader of the logic of the argument being presented, while at the same time providing a restatement, often with variations, of the component parts of the argument. Mustansir Mir was one of the first scholars to undertake literary analysis of the Qur'an, and in a 1986 article he identifies an elaborate mirror-image chiastic structure in surah 12 (*Joseph*), which as Rendsburg (1988) points out strongly parallels the chiastic structure of the Joseph story as it appears in Genesis. I raise this issue not because I want to imply that the Qur'an somehow copies the Torah, but rather to draw attention to just how common the use of chiasms was in early Semitic literature, especially in scriptural texts.

Similarly, it has been pointed out that surahs in the Qur'an appear to occur in natural pairs, as observed in the cases of surahs 73 and 74 (see chapter 2) and surahs 81 and 82 (see chapter 7). In both of these instances the adjacent surahs demonstrate similar structural characteristics, similar themes, and related use of language (vocabulary, syntax and so on). Combining the concept of a diptych with the idea that surahs appear in natural pairs, and adding in the notion of chiastic structure, I think that surahs 55 and 56 actually comprise what might be referred to as a chiastic diptych. In other words, not only do these two surahs form a natural pair, but they can also be viewed as two parts of a single thematic narrative, and the structure of the two surahs reinforces the thematic content through an extended mirror image chiasm, almost giving the impression that they form one large surah. Observations on the structure of these surahs by other scholars reinforce this interpretation.

Primarily on linguistic grounds, Robinson (2003: 135-38) divides each of these surahs into two parts. From his perspective, the two sections of surah 55 end with the expression "full of majesty, bestowing honor" in verses 27 and 78, while the two sections of surah 56 end with the expression "the Supreme" at verses 74 and 96. This scheme serves to divide the content of surah 55 basically in a ratio of one-third to two-thirds and the content of surah 56 in a ratio of two-thirds to one-third, thus establishing a structural symmetry between the two surahs, at least on a large scale. He goes on to divide these major sections into a number of smaller units based to some extent on thematic content, but also reflecting shifts in the tone of the language used – a feature he refers to as registers (125-26).

Employing a more thematic approach, Haleem (1999: 162) divides surah 55 into three parts, with the first part (1-30) described as dealing with the bounties of this world. He refers to the second part of the surah (31-45) as a challenge to those who think they can escape judgment, and he includes in this section the verses dealing with those who will go to hell. Haleem's third section (46-77) is outlined in terms of the bounties in the world to come, with verse 78 constituting a concluding remark. While he does not offer a structural outline for surah 56, he does draw attention to the structural parallels between the two surahs throughout his discussions, especially when describing the gardens (180).

Schematically, I would propose the following overall structure for surahs 55 and 56:

Surah 55

Signs (1-28)
Polemic (29-36)
Eschatology (37-78)
        Hell (43-44)
        Paradise (46-77)
                Greater (46-60)
                Lesser (61-77)
Concluding directive (78)

Surah 56

First reflection (1-74)
>   Eschatology (1-48)
>   >   Greater paradise (11-26)
>   >   Lesser paradise (27-40)
>   >   Hell (41-44)
>   Polemic (49-56)
>   Signs (57-73)
>   Concluding directive (74)

Second reflection (75-96)
>   Signs (75-80)
>   Polemic (81-87)
>   Eschatology (88-94)
>   >   Greater paradise (88-89)
>   >   Lesser paradise (90-91)
>   >   Hell (92-94)
>   Concluding directive (95-96)

The thematic order of surah 55 is signs-polemic-eschatology, with this order being reversed to eschatology-polemic-signs in the portion of surah 56 that I refer to as the first reflection. In the second reflection section of surah 56, the order of the first reflection is reversed and we return to the original order as presented in surah 55. I think that this final reversal is a signal to the reader to treat the contents of the second reflection as a summary of what has been presented in the previous 152 verses (the 78 verses of surah 55 plus the first 76 verses of surah 56). My choice of the terms signs, polemic and eschatology come from Robinson, but they also match quite well to Haleem's analysis, if we think of signs as bounties in this world, polemic as challenge, and eschatology representing the description of the world to come.

Even though surah 56 contains a greater number of verses than surah 55, the overall length of these two surahs is about the same, and the number of verses in the first reflection portion of surah 56 is approximately equal to the number of verses in surah 55. Both surahs are constructed using what are sometimes referred to in grammatical analysis as "atomic sentences," which are concise statements containing a single idea or expression. For example, verses 28 through 40 in surah 56 are part of a single sentence, but this one sentence contains thirteen distinct components, each with its own verse number, giving the impression of what we would now refer to as a series of bullet points.

In the three sections that follow I focus primarily on structural issues raised in the major thematic divisions of these two surahs, rather than on content. However, I do provide an analysis of a couple of passages as a means of demonstrating the way in which structural interpretation can influence theological understanding. A fourth section provides a description of three special aspects of surah 55.

Signs

We have become accustomed, at least from the standpoint of the intellectual heritage of the West, to think dualistically, separating body and mind, or the material

139

from the non-material. This sort of dualism entered our worldview through the musings of the 17th-century French philosopher Descartes with his famous observation, *cogito ergo sum* (I think therefore I am). While this kind of strict separationist dualism might dominate our ways of thinking in the modern world, especially when it is reinforced by the one/zero binary logic of digital technologies, dualism more generally appears as an integral structural feature of the natural world. We observe sun and moon, day and night, male and female, and even our bodies demonstrate duality with two ears, two eyes, two hands, and so on. This naturalistic dualism is characterized by complementarity rather than opposition or exclusion. Pairs of objects exist together in a relationship grounded in the affirmation of both rather than either/or. From this perspective, we should not be surprised when the wonders of creation are presented to us in pairs, in these surahs and elsewhere in the Qur'an.

The pairs of objects also have a broader cosmological significance. For example, verse 17 of surah 55 states: "He is Lord of the two risings and Lord of the two settings." As Haleem (2005: 353) suggests, this verse can be understood as referring to the rising and setting points of the sun and moon, or it might be referring to the rising and setting of the sun in winter and summer. It is perfectly reasonable to accept the idea that both of these meanings were intended, as both draw attention to natural cosmic phenomena and to our experience of them as the passage of time, whether on the scale of day-to-day, or season-to-season. It is not the mere existence of these pairs that is important, but also the dynamic interplay between the complementary elements.

In the second reflection portion of surah 56, verses 77 to 80 contain the four-part statement that "this is truly a noble Qur'an, in a protected Record that only the purified can touch, sent down from the Lord of all being." The third part of this statement has traditionally been interpreted to suggest that Muslims literally must not handle the Qur'an unless they are in a state of ritual purity, having performed the prescribed ablutions. Taking these verses at face value, I would suggest that the first and fourth parts of the statement provide a reiteration of the opening verses of surah 55, simultaneously establishing both an earthly manifestation and a divine origin for the Qur'an. Similarly, I think that the second and third parts of the statement, which in my view are inseparable, refer particularly to the timeless and transcendent quality of the Qur'an, and that it is only the pure of heart, especially those selected by God as prophets, that can "touch" the Qur'an – the word touch in this instance implying a recipient or vessel for transmitting the message. In other words, I am suggesting that this sequence of verses should be interpreted spiritually rather than materially. Remember that the Qur'an was revealed to the Prophet and distributed to the community orally, and it was not until twenty years after the death of Muhammad that the written text of the Qur'an was compiled. The spiritual intent of these verses (77 to 80) is reiterated in verse 95, emphasizing that the message contained in these verses (the whole Qur'an) is the certain truth – truth being timeless and transcendent. Based on this interpretation,

I think it is fair to suggest that the second reflection can be viewed not just as a summary of the content of the two surahs, but also as a succinct commentary on the opening verses of surah 55.

Polemic

As with the word diptych, the word polemic is Greek in origin implying hostility or opposition, and it is commonly used to signify a verbal dispute or argument. Polemical passages in the Qur'an often take the form of threats or challenges, but they can also appear as rhetorical questions. The polemic in surah 55 is contained in a specific series of challenges contained in verses 29 to 36, but more generally a polemic thread runs through the entire surah directed against humans and jinn, as evidenced in the refrain found first in verse 13, and then found 30 more times throughout the surah. The refrain, "Which, then, of your Lord's blessings do you both deny?" takes the form of a rhetorical question and is presented using the dual. In other words, as we saw in the previous chapter, the expression "you both" refers to two beings that are to be treated as one. Humans and jinns are simultaneously different and the same. They are different in that humans are made of clay (38:71), and jinns were made "from the fire of scorching wind" (15:27). They are the same in that they are the only two of God's creatures on Earth that are aware of their own existence. All other aspects of creation submit to the will of God by their very nature. For humans and jinns, submission is a conscious act, and therefore one that can be questioned. So, in surah 55, God questions the questioners, while presenting for their consideration all those aspects of creation that cannot be questioned.

The polemic sections in surah 56 are more directly related to eschatology, especially challenging those who deny judgment and life after death. Unlike the situation in surah 55, there is no continuous polemical thread running through the surah, and the intended audience is strictly human. The jinns are never mentioned in surah 56.

Eschatology

In surah 55 the discussion of hell is tied in with the polemic section against those who deny judgment. As verse 46 indicates, for those who fear the coming judgment there are two gardens. Later in verse 62, two more gardens are mentioned. These two latter gardens are described as being below the first pair of gardens, and the features of these two lower gardens appear to be less grandiose that those of the first two gardens. There is no indication that some people will inhabit the first gardens while others will inhabit the lower ones. The explicit distinction between the greater and lesser gardens, and the fact that different classes of people will inhabit these gardens, is only made in surah 56. Before moving on to surah 56 however, some clarification needs to be made with respect to the actual number of gardens being referred to.

Maintaining a strict dualism, we would anticipate

one hell and one garden (paradise), and at least in terms of human destiny surah 55 only designates two fates for people – hell or paradise. Similar to the situation discussed above regarding the rising and setting of the sun and moon, the mention of two gardens might be a mechanism to describe being surrounded by a garden just as the sun surrounds us through the day. Perhaps in the geographic context of the Arab people, the expression two gardens could be seen as a contrast to the image of an oasis – a single point of refuge surrounded by desert. In this sense, the gardens are like an oasis on all sides, with no encroaching sands. Similarly, the second pair of gardens might reflect the fact that no matter how far you wander from the heart of the first gardens, there will be gardens below these, and we might conjecture even further pairs of gardens beyond those.

Verse 7 of surah 56 indicates that people will be sorted into three classes, but I would suggest that the terms used to designate these three groups demonstrate that we are dealing not with a set of three equivalent choices, but rather with a set of nested dualisms. Visualizing this situation, here is what a literal three-option system would look like:

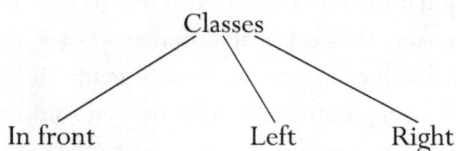

Classes

In front   Left   Right

Left and right appear as logical alternatives, but the idea of being out in front appears to insert a new cos-

Robert A. Campbell

mological element. In other words it alters our expectation of how creation is ordered, if for no other reason than we would expect that if some people are in front then some people must be behind. I think that the situation should be pictured this way:

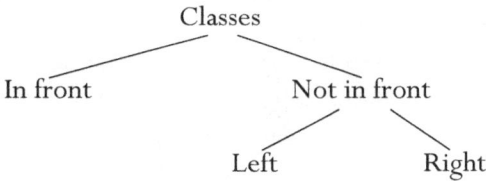

```
                    Classes
          /                    \
    In front              Not in front
                          /          \
                      Left            Right
```

The Qur'an does not speak of those who are behind. Rather, it goes directly to dividing those who are not in front into either left or right. Verse 13 particularly appears to suggest that those in front are a very select group that includes "many from the past." I would suggest that the Qur'an seems to be implying that these people are above the more mundane dualism of left and right. In other words, their lives are beyond reproach – almost transcending judgment. Perhaps this classification is reserved for prophets, or for those who accepted God without having to be warned. Whatever the case might be, my objective is to demonstrate that the dualistic thread of surahs 55 and 56, as well as of the rest of the Qur'an for that matter, is maintained in these verses even in the face of what appears at first glance to be evidence to the contrary.

Uniqueness of Surah 55

Even though the pairing of surahs has been emphasized throughout this chapter, it is interesting to note that surah 55 is unique among all the surahs in the Qur'an in that it begins with one of the beautiful names of God, it is addressed to both humans and jinns, and it contains a refrain.

Haleem (1999: 163) points out that not only is this the only surah that begins with one of the 99 beautiful names of God (see chapter 3), but the way in which the name is used establishes a very different relationship between God and the Qur'an than is normally expressed in the Qur'an. In surah 55, God teaches the Qur'an rather than engaging in the more commonly expressed action of sending it down (e.g., 16:64, 25:6). The Lord of Mercy is performing an act of mercy (teaching), thus dramatically drawing attention to the notion that the Qur'an has a dual nature – it is a warning, but it is also a mercy. I would suggest that the use of the divine name as subject in this instance implies that people should see the Qur'an first and foremost as a mercy.

The English word genie comes from the word jinn, and these beings are quite familiar to most people from the popular story of Aladdin and other tales that have come down to us as part of the collection known as the *One Thousand and One Arabian Nights* (Irwin 2003). As Chabbi (2003) explains, the jinns were an integral part of Arab folklore long before the beginnings of Islam and they remain so to the present day, even though their powers appear to be much diminished. I have already mentioned above what I see as the relationship between humans and jinns, and between this pair and the rest of creation. The significance of the fact that this surah is addressed to humans and jinns is that the consistency of everything appearing in pairs is maintained. Further, it provides a stark contrast to surah 56, in which the jinns are not present.

The idea of a refrain is taken from the analysis of poetic and musical works, and is used to identify a verse or verses that are repeated at regular intervals throughout a composition. The refrain in surah 55 occurs 31 times, and, with the exception of its first appearance in verse 13, it is placed after each listing of pairs of objects (Haleem 1999: 168). Whereas poetic refrains are often used to aid memory and provide a sense of regularity and familiarity, in this case I think the use of the refrain more closely parallels the repeated use of the word when in the short eschatological surahs examined in the previous chapter. The refrain addressed to humans and jinns is designed to create a sense of anxiety, impatience and intolerance, much like the mood that can be created in parents when a child on a long journey, forever asks: "Are we there yet?"

Haleem (1999: 181-83) points out that some scripture scholars have suggested that the structure of surah 55 is a direct imitation of Psalm 136, based on the observation that both texts contain a refrain, both are thematically about mercy, and both refer to great wonders. Here is a portion of Psalm 136, as it appears in the King James Version:

To him who alone doeth great wonders;

for his mercy endureth for ever.
To him that by wisdom made the heavens;
    for his mercy endureth for ever.
To him that stretched out the earth above the waters;
    for his mercy endureth for ever.
To him that made great lights;
    for his mercy endureth for ever. (136:4-7)

Careful analysis of these two texts quickly demonstrates that there are far more differences than similarities between them, but the more important point has to do with the quest to prove that the Qur'an is for the most part a derivative or imitative text. We have noted several parallels between the Qur'an and the Torah over the last several chapters, but this fact does not provide adequate grounds to suggest copying. The Hebrews and Arabs are both Semitic peoples, and their scriptures clearly identify their cultural and linguistic commonalities, as well as their shared belief in the same God. We should be more concerned and even alarmed if parallels did not exist.

Numerology

The number two has certainly played a prominent role in the discussions in this chapter and, as Rippin points out (2003: 550), in the Qur'an, the number two expresses the natural and perfect order of things, whether husband and wife, day and night, or the pairing of animals that Noah took on the ark (11:40). On the other hand, the number three appears to imply plurality, as in three days of fasting to overcome legal troubles

(5:89), the people of Salih being allowed three days to enjoy life before judgment was passed on them (11:65) and the condemnation of those who worship three gods (4:171). Four is associated with legal matters, as with four witnesses being required for accusations of adultery (4:15), and the four sacred months, during which certain activities such as waging war are forbidden (9:2). At the same time, Rippin observes that the number eight, used about five times in the Qur'an, appears to have no unifying symbolic value (2003: 552).

This latter observation should serve to remind us that we need to be careful not to over-interpret every aspect of the text. However, I think it is fair to suggest that the use of particular numbers in the Qur'an is neither arbitrary nor merely literal. In every culture, numbers have a symbolic content that conveys a layer of meaning that goes beyond what the literal numeric character designates. In other words, there is something of broader significance conveyed in the concept of "two-ness" that is not conveyed simply by the concept two, and the Arabs hearing the message of Qur'an for the first time would have understood this.

I am particularly fascinated by the use of prime numbers in the Qur'an. A prime number is a number that has exactly two natural number divisors – itself and one (e.g., 2, 3, 5, 7, 11, 13, 17, 19, 23, 29, 31 and so on). Clearly, the use of the prime numbers below ten is quite common throughout the Qur'an, and the use of the number seven, for example, to express items of cosmic significance, such as the seven heavens (17:44), is consistent with its use in much Near Eastern thought (Rippin 2003: 552). However, the use of prime numbers greater than ten is much more rare and rather thought provoking. The number eleven is used only once in the Qur'an, in reference to the eleven stars that bowed down to Joseph in his dream (12:4). This particular example of the use of a prime number is probably the easiest to explain, as it corresponds to the number of Joseph's brothers. However, less easy to explain is the use of the number nineteen as the number of guardians of the gates of hell (74:30) and, as discussed above, the indirect use of the number 31 as the number of times the refrain in surah 55 appears. Whether there is any special significance to the fact that these are prime numbers is a matter of pure speculation.

The term gematria, which is related to other words of Greek origin such as geometry that are used to express the idea of measurement, refers to the mystical practice of discovering the hidden meaning of texts by transforming the letters of the alphabet into corresponding numbers (Schimmel 1993). Varisco (2003: 554) points out that at various times Muslims have practised gematria as part of healing rituals, in interpreting the Qur'an, and in divination – the art of foretelling the future or discovering hidden knowledge (see Fahd 2001). The substitution table for converting letters to numbers is based on the order of letters in the old Semitic alphabet (e.g., a=1, b=2, j=3, d=4, h=5, and so on). So, for example, when the nineteen letters of the *basmalah* are transformed into their corresponding numbers and then added together, the sum is 786. The use of 786 as a sort of numerical shorthand for the *basmalah* appears to be fairly common practice in various aspects of popular cultural expression, especially among Muslims in India and Pakistan (Freitag 2007). Systematic explorations of the origins and significance of this and related practices however are sorely lacking.

9

The Longest Surah
(Qur'an 2)

As I stated at the outset, I think it is instructive both to read the Qur'an and to understand the emergence of Islam against the background of competing monotheisms, rather than solely against a background of idolatry, polytheism or ignorance. I am not suggesting that Muhammad and the early Islamic community did not have to struggle against the moral, political, social and religious traditions of the Arab people. However, I think that this particular struggle was mostly physical (material) in nature, manifesting itself in inter-tribal economic disputes characterized by trade embargoes, caravan raids and the occasional outright battle. Certainly from a contemporary perspective, and especially since the events of September 11, 2001, I think we have become over sensitized to this primarily materialistic interpretation of jihad (struggle). What I am suggesting in this book is that the more theological and faith-based struggle faced by the early Muslims was one in which the religious traditions and scripture of the Jews and Christians would be relatively familiar and probably quite well understood. Notwithstanding the obvious reverence for Mary and Jesus illustrated in the Qur'an, Christianity as a religious system would likely pose the smallest threat to the early spread of Islam, as the doctrine of the Trinity could easily be interpreted and denounced as polytheistic. Judaism on the other hand was clearly monotheistic and, as I have already remarked (see chapter 5), I think it is plausible to suggest that many Arabs hearing Muhammad's message for the first time might ask: "Why not just become Jews?"

In this chapter and the next, I explore the way in which the message of the Qur'an reflects the tension between trying to retain an essential historical and theological continuity with those who had previously heeded God's message, and the need to establish a unique identity for those who upon hearing the message delivered by Muhammad now chose to submit to God's will. This delicate balance of continuity and differentiation that describes the relationship between Jews and Muslims is contrasted with the more blatant differentiation and explicit discontinuity that would be established with respect to the pagan Arabs.

As might be expected, the longest surah in the Qur'an offers extended discussions on almost every issue it deals with. It is impossible in one chapter, or even one book of this length, to provide a thorough coverage of even a limited amount of its content. Consequently, I have chosen to focus on a few small sections of the surah, as well as providing in-depth coverage of a couple of individual verses. I begin with a brief discussion of the overall thematic structure of the surah.

Thematic Structure

The longest surah in the Qur'an, referred to as *The Cow* (2), is composed of 286 verses, comprising about one-twelfth or eight percent of the total length of the Qur'an. It contains the longest single verse in the Qur'an (2:282), and it also contains the well-known "Throne verse" (2:255), which through time has been incorporated into several aspects of Islamic piety and popular culture (e.g., Hatley 2007). The designation of the surah comes from the reference in verses 67 through 71 to a story found in the book of Numbers (19), pertaining to the criteria by which the Hebrew people were to select a particular cow for the purpose of sacrifice. As Robinson (2003: 201) indicates, the story of the cow is not of great significance within the surah; rather the naming of the surah probably just reflects the fact that the Arabic word for cow (*baqarah*) appears here four times and nowhere else in the Qur'an.

Robinson (2003: 202-203) suggests that the surah can be divided into five major sections, followed by a brief epilogue, as follows:

Even though this surah does not present a contiguous historical narrative, it does to some extent follow a chronological ordering of themes, moving from Adam up to the period very close to the end of the Prophet's life when, having established a Muslim community in Madina, it was time to reclaim the city of Makkah and the Ka'bah for Islam.

In chapter 1, I used the shortest surah (108) to illustrate the commonly employed three-part thematic structure comprised of two contrasting sections separated by a conditional. I would suggest that the longest surah in the Qur'an also follows this format. The first 141 verses of the surah constitute the negative side of the contrast, in that they deal with the way in which previous responses to God's message have failed. The conditional section in verses 142 to 152 establishes the change in the direction of prayer from Jerusalem to Makkah as the definitive demarcation between the Muslims and those who had gone before. The remaining verses constitute the positive aspect, indicating what the expanding Islamic community needs to do in response to God's message in order to succeed in this world and the next.

Surah 2 begins with three detached letters, and as I stated a couple of times in earlier chapters, I have saved a discussion of the meaning of these letters until this point.

Alif Lam Mim

Throughout the Qur'an there are 29 surahs that begin with what are referred to alternately as detached, isolated or abbreviated letters. Fourteen letters of the Arabic alphabet are used in this way, and individual surahs begin with between one and five of these letters in various combinations. Surah 42 (*Consultation*) is unique in this regard in that it begins with two sets of isolated letters, *ha mim* in verse 1 and *ayn sin qaf* in verse 2. Surah 2 begins with the letters *alif lam mim*, as do surahs 3, 29, 30, 31 and 32. Whether there is any special significance to the fact that these six surahs share this letter combination is a matter of speculation, as is the matter of the meaning of these letters altogether.

Over the centuries, Muslim and non-Muslim commentators have made a number of suggestions as to the correct interpretation of these letters (Massey 2003). Among these are the opinions that they are alternate names for the Qur'an, one of the names of God, or the title of the surah to which they are attached. On a more material cultural level scholars have suggested that the use of these letters is linked to the development of writing, as the fourteen letters used for this purpose actually constitute the original graphemes (letter symbols) found in the Arabic alphabet prior to the Islamic period. Among the mystical interpretations of these letters are suggestions that the meaning is a secret, that the use of these letters was a means of tricking the polytheists into listening to the Qur'an, and that the true meaning can only be derived through gematria – converting the letters to their numerical equivalents (see chapter 8). From a contemporary perspective, not only is their meaning and significance unclear, but the debate also continues over whether these letters should even be considered as part of the Qur'an.

Irfan Shahid (2004: 418) relates that, while some scholars view these letters as an editorial addition from the time of the Uthmanic compilation of the Qur'an some 20 years after the death of Muhammad, the majority of Muslim and non-Muslim scholars view these letters as part of the original revelation. Shahid is of the opinion that these letters represent portions of the revelation that the Prophet did not hear clearly and so rather than leave them out, or try to interpret what God intended by these sounds, Muhammad simply related them exactly as he heard them and then recited them accordingly. While this theory celebrates the veracity of the Prophet with respect to his delivery of the revelations without alteration, it might also be taken to imply that part of the message of the Qur'an is missing.

Taking a more linguistically based perspective that focuses on the Qur'an as a recitation, Robinson (2003: 203) observes that the three letters at the beginning of this surah represent three distinct locations with respect to the physiological origins of their sound – *alif* in the throat, *lam* in the mouth and *mim* on the lips. In this sense, the sequence of letters reflects the physical action of reciting – of bringing forth the sound of the Qur'an.

The Prologue (1-39)

The prologue to the second surah is longer than more than half of the surahs in the Qur'an, and consistent with Haleem's (2005: 4-7) division of these 39 verses into paragraphs, the thematic structure of the prologue can be outlined as follows:

Detached letters (1)
Believers and non-believers (2-7)
Hypocrites (8-20)
Creation (21-24)
Eschatology (25)
Covenant (26-29)
Adam (30-33)
Iblis/Satan (34-39)

Given the broad range of topics covered in the prologue, it is fair to suggest that these verses provide an introduction to the entire contents of the Qur'an. At the same time, the prologue begins with a direct link back to the request for guidance in *The Opening*, when it declares in verse 2 that this book contains guidance. However, it adds the condition that this guidance is available for those "who are mindful of God."

Yusuf Ali (2004: 17) suggests that this expression is intended to convey the notion of acquiring knowledge, as alluded to in the Hebrew book of Proverbs

1:7, where it states: "The fear of the Lord is the beginning of knowledge." Consistent with this interpretation, Yusuf Ali translates this conditional portion of the verse to read: "those who fear Allah." However, he also mentions that the same Arabic root word (*taqwa*) that he translates as fear can be interpreted to imply restraint from evil thoughts and actions, or behaving and acting righteously. Given these comments and taking context in to account, I do not think that the intention of this phrase is to suggest that people should be afraid of God, but rather that they should be wary of God – that they should act in the knowledge that God knows what they do. It is interesting to note that the expression is used again twice at the end of this surah (verses 282 and 283) with reference to those who might consider failing to meet the obligations of a business transaction.

Several verses (8 to 20) are devoted to a description of the hypocrites – those who say one thing and do something else. I think it is fair to imagine that some people would see economic, social or political advantage in being counted among the believers in some instances and among the non-believers at other times. However, it is unlikely that these verses are suggesting that there are three classes of people, each destined to meet their own fate. Rather, from the content of these verses, I think it is obvious that the hypocrites will be counted among the non-believers.

The account of the creation of Adam as a successor (verse 30) and his being taught the names of things by God (verse 31) provides a starting point for the historical thread that runs through the rest of the surah, while at the same time establishing the fundamental characteristics that describe the relationship between God and humankind. What I want to focus on at this point is the response to Adam's creation by one of the angels.

In a number of places throughout the Qur'an such as 7:10-25 and 17:53-65 (see chapter 10), Iblis and Satan are mentioned together, raising the question of whether these are two names for the same being, or whether these are two distinct beings. Based on the account presented in surah 2, Iblis clearly existed before Adam, and it is only as a result of God's command for the angels to bow down before Adam that Iblis rebels. Further, it is only when humans are living out their lives, having been instructed by God, that Satan is allowed to tempt them away from God. From this I would conclude that there is no need to determine the precise existential relationship between Iblis and Satan, if in fact such a thing was possible. Rather, I think that the alternate names have a purely rhetorical function that aids the reader in understanding the message of the Qur'an. When the intended meaning of the text is to draw attention to the fact that the creation of humans was of such significance that it caused an angel to rebel, the name Iblis is used. When the intention is to highlight the fact that in spite of the status afforded them by God humans are weak and can be tempted away from God, the name Satan is used. Simply put, Iblis stands for rebellion and Satan stands for temptation.

The Direction of Prayer (142-152)

As stated above, the central section of this surah establishes the condition of changing the direction of prayer from Jerusalem to Makkah, or more specifically from Solomon's Temple to the Ka'bah, a structure completed by Abraham and Ishmael (2:127). The importance of the condition is emphasized through multiple references to the change including, in verses 149 and 150, a literal repetition of the command to turn in a new direction. However, this section also contains another reference that is critical to understanding the overall interpretation of this surah.

The numerical center of the second surah occurs at verse 143, which contains the phrase "just community," or as Yusuf Ali translates it, "an *ummah* (community) justly balanced" (2004: 58). As will be discussed below, the notion of a balanced community can be viewed as an example of the commonly used mercantile analogy, but at this point I want to concentrate on how the idea of a balanced community might be related to the idea of a new focal point for prayer. Taking the word balanced to imply centered or intermediate, Yusuf Ali points out that Arabia was geographically centered among the civilizations of the Old World, and that the position of the Islamic community as an intermediary is witnessed by its expansion in all directions. From my perspective this interpretation reads too much later history back into the text of the Qur'an, but it does suggest an interesting observation about establishing identity.

With Jerusalem as the focal point, people in Makkah or Madina would roughly be facing the same direction (slightly west of north) during prayer. This action would create a sort of perceptual contradiction, whereby, in spite of the existence of a new messenger and a message directed towards a new community, access to God would still appear to be distant in space and time. With the shift to the Ka'bah as focal point, access to God becomes immediate and local. Praying from Madina, people would now point south towards the heart of Arab cultural heritage. Within Makkah, it would be possible, depending on where one was in the city, to face north, south, east or west, and still be facing the right (just) direction for prayer.

The interpretation that these verses constitute a conditional section with respect to the overall three-part structure of the surah is further reinforced by the additional exchange relationship established in the last two verses (151 and 152). God sent a messenger to purify people, give them a scripture and teach them things they did not know, and people are instructed to remember God and be thankful to Him.

The Throne Verse (255)

As mentioned above, the "Throne verse" is one of the best-known and most cherished verses in the Qur'an. We can gain some appreciation of the high esteem in which this verse is held from Yusuf Ali's (2004) rather philosophical observation: "Who can translate its glorious meaning, or reproduce the rhythm of its well-

chosen and comprehensive words? Even in the original
Arabic the meaning seems to be greater than can be expressed in words" (105). What is it about this verse that
can generate such an aura of reverence and awe? I would
suggest that, at least in part, the evocative power of this
verse emerges out of the fact that it demonstrates one of
the most effective uses of chiastic structure in the whole
Qur'an. Here is the complete text of the verse divided
into the components of the chiasm.

Preface – God, there is no god but Him,
A – the Ever Living, the Ever Watchful.
  B – Neither sleep nor slumber overtakes Him.
   C – All that is in the heavens and in the earth
    belongs to Him.
    D –Who is there that can intercede with Him
     except by His leave?
     E – He knows what is before them and
      what is behind them,
    D' – but they do not comprehend any of His
     knowledge except what He wills.
   C' – His throne extends over the heavens and
    the earth;
  B' – it does not weary Him to preserve them both.
A' – He is the Most High, the Tremendous.

The thematic symmetry of this verse can be outlined as follows: Oneness of God (preface), divine
names (A-A'), tiredness and sleep (B-B'), creation and
majesty (C-C'), God's will (D-D'), and knowing humanity (E).

The preface performs a number of functions, the first of which is to set this verse apart from the verses that precede and follow it. Further, not only does this prefatory phrase contain a reiteration of the central theological message of the Qur'an (namely, the Oneness of God), but it also serves to set up the expectation that in what follows we will learn something important about God. Having identified the opening phrase as a preface, it is quite easy to observe the way in which the remaining phrases align into complementary pairs, pointing towards a central phrase (E), the message of which is that God's knowledge is not only about the past history of humanity, but also about its future. The obvious question that emerges at this point then is determining what any of this has to do with a throne.

Perhaps, in a similar fashion to the way in which surah 2 takes its name from the fact the Arabic word for cow appears only in this surah, the "Throne verse" gets its name from the fact that this is the only place in the Qur'an where God's throne is mentioned. However, this is not the case. The issue is much more complex.

Thomas O'Shaughnessy (1973) identifies 22 places where God's throne is referred to in the Qur'an, but in all but one of these instances the word that is translated as throne is Arabic in origin (*arsh*). In the "Throne verse," the word that is used for throne is an Aramaic loanword, *kursi*. However, the word *kursi* is used in another location in the Qur'an (38:34), where it refers to Solomon's throne: "We certainly tested Solomon, reducing him to a mere skeleton on his throne." The question to be answered then appears to be one of determining the way in which this particular reference to God's throne is different from the 21 other instances in the Qur'an in which God's throne is mentioned, and of identifying the common factor between God's throne and Solomon's throne that further clarifies the use of this particular loanword.

Omar (2001: 483) suggests that the word *kursi* can be translated as authority or knowledge rather than literally as throne. Thus, the use of this word draws attention to the attributes associated with the one who occupies the throne, rather than to the chair itself. Based on this interpretation, substituting the word "authority" for the word "throne" (C') would clearly be a logical match for the word "belongs" (C). At the same time, when the use of the word *kursi* in this verse is compared to its use in 38:34, a double-layered contrast is established between God and Solomon and between Solomon and other people. Solomon was singled out by God to have power over the wind and the jinn (38:36-37), and he was even given the ability to speak to the birds (27:16). His throne (knowledge and authority) extended well beyond that which God granted to other mortals, even to other prophets. By contrast God's throne (knowledge and authority) is that much greater still, extending over all aspects of creation. The image of Solomon as a skeleton reinforces the magnitude of this contrast by pointing to the physical frailty of mere humans.

Within the context of this verse, the use of the word kursi also suggests that there is a broader cosmological significance associated with the concept of God's

throne. God is transcendent in that He stands outside
of creation and is not bound by the physical constraints
(e.g., sleep) that are a daily reminder to humans of
their weakness. At the same time, God is immanent
to the extent that He takes an active role in the eternal
unfolding of the created order and has an ongoing relationship with humanity, the pinnacle of creation. This
paradox of divine existence establishes a stark contrast
with pagan gods that were represented by stone effigies
and existed in particular locations. Similarly, it serves
to remind people that God is for all time and yet no
time, and for all place and yet no place. God is beyond
place (space) and time. These constraints apply only to
humans and other aspects of creation.

I think that one of the reasons that this verse is
identified as the "Throne verse" and why it is so well
known and revered is that it provides a strong theological counterpoint to the central message of this surah
regarding the change in direction of prayer. With all
of the importance given to repatriating the Ka'bah and
establishing it as the focal point of Muslim prayer, the
hazard existed for people to view the Ka'bah as God's
throne, or literally as the place where God resides.
The "Throne verse" functions as a cautionary tale, re-
minding people that it is only they who are confined to
spatial and temporal existence. The Ka'bah was made
for people, not people for the Ka'bah. To the extent
that humans persist in trying to find God at a certain
place and a certain time, they miss the opportunity to
experience God at all times and in all places.

As a final note on this subject, it is interesting to observe that the preface and initial set of divine names (A) used in this verse appear as the opening verses of surah 3, thus not only highlighting the central importance of the "Throne verse," but also providing an explicit link between these two long adjacent surahs, in a sense building the expectation that what follows in the third surah will provide a further explication of God's knowledge of the past and future of His creation.

The Longest Verse (282)

Clearly one verse or another in the Qur'an has to be the longest verse, and the fact that the longest verse occurs in the longest surah should not be surprising, nor might it be of any particular significance. However, there are two interconnected features of this verse that make it noteworthy for analysis. First, this verse employs a mercantile analogy, which as we observed previously (chapter 7) is a common literary mechanism used in the Qur'an when judgment and other eschatological themes are being discussed. Second, as Robinson (2003: 220-21) points out, the words "writing" and "scribe" occur no less than four times each in this verse.

On first reading, verse 282 appears to contain straightforward advice on the proper method for recording a business transaction. There must be a certain number of witnesses present and the transaction should be written down. At the same time, the placement of this verse very near the end of the surah produces an interesting counterpoint to the mercantile reference near the beginning of the surah where we read about the hypocrites who "bought error in exchange for guidance, so their trade reaps no profit" (2:16). The presence of witnesses and the fact that an agreement is put in writing act to prevent unscrupulous individuals from saying one thing and doing something else.

The repeated reference to scribes draws attention to the fact that at the time of the revelation of the Qur'an Arab culture was still for the most part oral. The number of scribes available to record business transactions or produce any other form of document was likely quite limited. Perhaps part of the message of this verse is to give notice of the need for more scribes and to signal that with the Qur'an Arab culture was shifting from a past remembered through oral tradition to a future guided by the written word.

Consistent with this interpretation, I think it is also fair to suggest that the repeated reference to writing provides a justification for establishing the practice of writing down the Qur'an, so that it will not be misinterpreted or forgotten. In the middle of the verse, writing down a debt is described as "more equitable in God's eyes, more reliable as testimony, and more likely to prevent doubt arising between you." Each of these conditions can be used to describe the Qur'an. The Qur'an strikes a balance between being a book of guidance and one of warning, thus providing the basis for a balanced or middle community as discussed above. Similarly, regarding faithful testimony, we might conceive of the prophets as God's witnesses and the Qur'an as a contract of debt between humanity and God. Finally, as emphasized in the "Throne verse", God has knowledge of the weaknesses of humanity and the fact that people can be tempted, an understanding that is reinforced in this verse when it mentions that a debtor may be "feeble minded."

Thematically, verse 283 should be read in conjunction with the longest verse. To some, verse 283 might appear as an interpolation addressing the need to provide security (a deposit) when a person is on a journey and cannot find a scribe. However, I think that this verse is part of the original sequence of verses, which, as will be discussed in the next section, also includes verse 284. In part, I base my interpretation on the observation that the use of the phrase to be "mindful of God" provides an obvious link back to the use of this expression in verse 2, where the provision of guidance is linked to the condition of being wary of God – knowing that God knows. Consistent with this view, I would suggest that the notion of being on a journey does not mean literal travel, as much as it refers to the idea of being out of sight of those who would otherwise monitor your activities. Just as God's throne is not confined by space and time, the message of this verse is that there is no way to be outside of God's view.

The Epilogue (284–286)

Robinson places the last three verses of the surah together as an epilogue. Alternately in his translation, Haleem (2005: 33) places verse 284 together with the two previous verses thereby implying that this verse functions as a conclusion on the subject of the longest verse. Haleem's construction appears to make more sense thematically and structurally, aligning the structure of this sequence of verses with the pattern established in several of the prior sequences ending, for example, in verses 266, 273 and 281.

The two primary characteristics that appear to set verses 285 and 286 apart as an epilogue are the fact that they constitute a prayer, and that they shift the focus away from providing instructions on practical matters of everyday life towards a more theological reflection on God, His messengers and those who believe. One of the most striking components of this change of focus is the contrast established by the use of the phrase "We hear and obey" to describe the response of all the faithful as opposed to the phrase "We hear and we disobey," used in verse 93 in reference to the Hebrew people who rejected the commandments given by God to Moses.

When viewed as a prayer, the epilogue can be understood as a parallel to *The Opening*, with the two sequences (1:1-7 and 2:285-286) forming a more obvious prologue and epilogue to the second surah, with the first 39 verses of surah 2 actually constituting an introduction to, and summary of, what is to come. Thus, practical instruction and the establishment of a distinct Muslim identity (signalled by the change in direction of prayer) are bracketed by prayers through which the believers request guidance and seek to be differentiated from those who have failed to follow God's message in the past. The final words of the second surah return the reader to the final verses of *The Opening*: "Guide us to the straight path: the path of those You have blessed, those who incur no anger and who have not gone astray" (1:6-7).

10

The Middle Surah
(Qur'an 17)

In this final chapter I explore a number of issues that arise from reading surah 17, which stands roughly in the middle of the Qur'an. While I would not go so far as to suggest that this surah is somehow at the center of a large chiasm formed by the entire text of the Qur'an, I think it is interesting to note that the word Qur'an is used more often and the subject of the Qur'an is discussed more thoroughly in this surah than anywhere else in the Qur'an. Surah 17 is also one of only eight surahs in the Qur'an, the others being surahs 9, 40, 41, 68, 76, 94 and 111, that is referred to by alternate Arabic names. In translation, surah 17 is called either *The Night Journey*, or *The Children of Israel*. Even though the majority of scholars agree that the names of the surahs are for the most part arbitrary,

I think that both of the names used for surah 17 are highly suggestive of the content and importance of this surah. One of the major ideas discussed in the previous chapter is the notion of how the Qur'an reflects the need to maintain continuity with the Jews, while at the same time establishing a new and different identity for Muslims. Perhaps the fact that surah 17 is referred to by these particular alternate names reflects the tension between these two objectives. Aside from this, the concept of the night journey is especially interesting in its own right, and in what follows I explore the way in which the concept of a journey is used to clarify the roles of Muhammad and the Qur'an, as well as to increase our understanding of the relationship between God and humanity. In a brief concluding section I offer some final observations, not just about this chapter, but also about the book as a whole.

Structure

Robinson (2003: 188) emphasizes the difficulties that commentators face when trying to analyze this surah, when he observes that the surah has a discursive structure. His selection of this term is particularly insightful when we remember that the word discursive has two well-established meanings. On the one hand it is used as a synonym for the word rambling, suggesting the arbitrary movement from one topic to another with no apparent line of reasoning. On the other hand, it means to move from one aspect of an argument to another in a systematic or logical manner. Perhaps in this instance, as contrary as they might seem, both meanings are equally applicable. However, Robinson goes on to explain that, with the exception of the first verse, all of the verses in this surah end in the same rhyme. The significance of this observation is that linguistically the surah appears to be a unified work, but unlike the case with most other surahs where clustered patterns and variations in the rhyme scheme are used to reinforce the thematic content of the surah, in this case, it appears that the persistent repetition of a single rhyme serves to some degree to disguise or obscure the thematic content. While I think that Robinson makes some valuable points, I would suggest that his observations draw attention to the limitations of employing an overly "textualist" approach to studying the Qur'an, as opposed to the more "contextualist" approach that I have been trying to demonstrate throughout this book (see chapter 1). More specifically, I would suggest that sometimes paying too much attention to the peculiar nuances of the Arabic language can obscure the content of the verses being studied and perhaps prevent the reader from seeing how thematic elements in one surah are linked to ideas developed in other passages in that surah and throughout the Qur'an.

The following scheme provides one way of viewing the overall organization of the surah.

> Prelude (1)
> Prologue (2-3)
> Framing narrative (4-8)
> Thematic section (9-52)

Core message (53-65)
Thematic section (66-100)
Framing narrative (101-104)
Epilogue (105-111)

Leaving aside the prelude for a moment, this scheme
would appear to suggest that, at least on a large scale,
the surah displays a chiastic structure. However, this
impression is somewhat misleading. I do think that
there is a degree of symmetry apparent in the structure of the surah, especially with respect to the first
ten verses and last ten verses of surah, and with respect
to the middle section (verses 53 to 65). At the same
time, as will become clear below, the major thematic
sections of the surah do not fit neatly into a chiastic
pattern, nor do they appear to be consistent with the
type of three-part structure that we observed in surah
2 (see chapter 9).

Thematically, with the exception of the two portions that I identify as constituting the framing narrative, and again setting aside the prelude, the remaining sections of this surah all deal more or less directly
with some aspect of the Qur'an. I have separated out
the prologue and epilogue partially because they stand
outside the framing narrative, but also because they
serve the familiar functions that we have observed being associated with these structural components elsewhere in the Qur'an – namely, linking this surah with
the Qur'an more broadly and providing introductory
and summary material respectively. Similarly, I have
separated out the verses containing what I refer to as

the core message of the surah, because they do appear to demonstrate a more obvious and finely detailed chiastic structure pointing towards a central verse (60).

The Jews

In surah 17, the two sections devoted to the Jews function as a framing narrative (Abbott 2008) for the rest of the surah. Much like a prologue and epilogue the opening and closing portions of the framing narrative bracket the contents of the surah, but unlike a prologue and epilogue they signal to the reader that, rather than alluding to the primary focus of the surah, they contain a message that should be kept in the back of one's mind as one is reading through the surah. In the same way as I have suggested throughout this book that the emergence of Islam should be viewed against a background of competing monotheisms, this framing narrative appears to be suggesting that what this surah has to say about the Qur'an should be read in full knowledge of the fact that the message now being sent through Muhammad was revealed at an earlier time and on more than one occasion to the Jews.

In the opening sequence of the narrative (verses 4 to 8) we learn that two previous judgments have been passed against the Jews because they had become corrupt and arrogant. Commentators generally agree that the events alluded to in these verses are the destruction of the Temple in Jerusalem under Nebuchadnezzar and the Babylonians in 586 BCE and the final destruction of the Temple in 70 CE by the Romans under Titus. The verses also suggest that if the Jews continue in their errant ways they will be subject to a final damning judgment. Yusuf Ali (2004: 675) remarks that perhaps this third warning is referring to the opportunity for the Jews to accept the message delivered by Muhammad – an interesting counterpoint to the idea of the Arabs becoming Jews.

In the closing sequence of the narrative (verses 101 to 104), we learn that in spite of the clear signs from God presented to Pharaoh by Moses, Pharaoh was still intent on eliminating the Jews – a motive for which he and his people were drowned. God then saved the Jews and allowed them to prosper, bringing the law to them through Moses. Perhaps the broader message of the framing narrative is that it is God and not other humans who will determine the fate of nations and peoples. At the same time, when God chooses, certain nations will be allowed to prevail over other nations to carry out God's work. The Jews were saved from the Egyptians in order to receive God's message, and then, having failed to respond appropriately, they suffered at the hands of more than one enemy. By analogy, this narrative might be suggesting that the growing Muslim community will triumph over the pagan Arabs but that like the Jews, should they become corrupt and arrogant, the time might come when they will be punished by other nations or peoples, on God's behalf.

Idolatry

In the middle of what I have identified as the first thematic section, a long sequence of verses (22 to 38) is devoted to outlining a set of commandments that bear a strong resemblance to the Ten Commandments found in the Torah (Exodus 20:1-17). As important as these commandments might be in providing a code of conduct for the emerging Muslim community, I want to focus on the two verses that follow this sequence. Verses 39 and 40 form a coda that reiterates what is arguably the most important commandment, while also taking a familiar subject and transforming it into something of broader significance.

The term coda, based on the Latin word for tail, is used in the analysis of musical works to refer to a passage that is added on at the end of a composition. I am using the word coda in this instance because I want to differentiate the function of these verses from the function associated with an interpolation. As has been demonstrated in previous chapters, an interpolation is a later addition to the text of a surah that usually offers some explanation of the contents of the verse it follows. By contrast, a coda should be viewed as an integral part of the original composition that shares with an interpolation the function of adding further information. However, with a coda, rather than serving to clarify an issue, the new information is likely to add a greater degree of complexity to the message of the verses it follows.

Verse 39 repeats the monotheistic message of verse 22 to have no other gods but God, and regarding this portion of the message, the coda is simply reinforcing the significance of this particular commandment. What follows in verse 40 however, is a much differ-

179

ent matter. The tone becomes highly polemical and readers are confronted with the rhetorical question of whether God should give people sons while taking daughters for Himself from among the angels. Looking internally first, this message might be related to the commandment in verse 31 not to kill children for fear of poverty, although I am unclear as to what that link would be. Yusuf Ali (2004: 685) suggests that the reference to daughters should be interpreted as a sort of supreme insult to God, especially in light of the attitude towards female children at the time, but to my mind this interpretation is overly simplistic. Given the theological and structural sophistication of this surah, I think there is much more to it than that.

In my opinion, the fact that the daughters are linked to the angels suggests that what is being referred to in verse 40 are the pagan goddesses named in surah 53 (*The Star*), where in verses 19 and 20 we read: "[Disbelievers], consider al-Lat and al-Uzza, and the third one Manat." Clearly the fact that these idols are mentioned specifically by name in the Qur'an suggests that the Arab people would be very familiar with them and that they played an important role in the pre-Islamic religious life of the Arabs. This interpretation is further supported when we realize that the mention of these goddesses is associated with the controversy of the so-called "Satanic verses."

Most readers of this book will be aware of this term from the title of a 1988 novel by Salman Rushdie, which many Muslims interpreted as a thinly disguised and highly derogatory biography of the Prophet, and against which Ayatollah Khomeini issued a fatwa (judgment) calling for Rushdie's death, as well as the deaths of others involved in publishing and distributing this work. However, the controversy has a much longer history. According to tradition (Esack 2005: 44), right after the Prophet recited these verses naming these goddesses, Satan put the following words into Muhammad's mouth: "They are the Exalted Birds (high flying cranes) and their intercession is to be hoped for." Apparently, members of the Quraysh tribe, hearing these verses, thought that this was a concession to their pagan gods, and they willingly prostrated themselves after the recitation in recognition and acceptance of Muhammad's message. When Muhammad realized what had happened, he was very troubled, but God reassured him, saying that he was like all other prophets before him and that Satan had tempted them and confused their words, but that He would replace the words of Satan. The seven verses (53:21-27) revealed to replace the "Satanic verses" directly parallel the message of surah 17 verse 40 highlighting the absurdity of God having daughters.

Placing this coda within the broader thematic context of surah 17, I think that we are being presented with a brief but very explicit condemnation of idolatry and the pagan religion of the Arabs, that can be contrasted with the more elaborate and drawn out efforts to demonstrate that the relationship between the emerging Muslim community and the Jews is one of differentiation and continuity. There is further support for this interpretation elsewhere in the surah. Verse 42 is also polemical, stating that if there were other gods then surely they would have tried to find a way to the "Lord of the Throne." This appears to be a direct reference to the "Throne verse" (2:255), which, as was discussed in the previous chapter, presents an image of God as being everywhere and nowhere at the same time. This transcendent image forms a stark contrast to the fact that the false gods referred to can be found in a literal place – local shrines containing stone effigies.

The Qur'an

The content of the prologue and epilogue make it clear that the thematic focus of this surah is the Qur'an. The verses of the prologue mention that Moses was given the scripture, and I would suggest that this should be interpreted to mean that he received the same message as was now being revealed to Muhammad. In other words, this is not a reference to the Torah, as it would be known in the Prophet's time, but rather a reference to the fundamental message delivered to and through all of God's prophets. I think it is also significant that Noah is named in these verses, as he was the only one of his generation who listened to God and heeded the warning he was given.

In the epilogue, the point is made that the recitation was revealed in parts and that it should be recited to the people at intervals and only a little piece at a time. Not only does this advice form an interesting contrast to the statement made in verse 11 that "man is ever hasty," but it also emphasizes the oral and aural aspects of the Qur'an, reinforcing an image of God's message as vibrant and "on the air", rather than written down and stored on a shelf. This interpretation is supported by the advice in the verses that follow to be neither too loud nor too soft in saying prayers, but to seek a "middle way."

In the previous chapter, the idea of a middle community was discussed with reference to the change in the direction of prayer from Jerusalem to Makkah. In the epilogue of surah 17, the reference to the middle way could be taken to imply that while the Qur'an must be recited constantly, people cannot be forced to heed its message. Guidance and a warning are always available to those who will listen.

Continuing with this interpretive thread, verse 46 indicates that covers have been put on the hearts of the non-believers so that they cannot understand the message of the Qur'an. Whatever message this verse contains about predestination and free will is an interesting problem in its own right, but I would identify this statement as a direct link to the claim in surah 56 verse 79 that only the pure of heart can touch the Qur'an (see chapter 8).

The Core Message

As mentioned above, I do not think that surah 17 demonstrates an overall chiastic structure, nor does it illustrate the sort of three-part structure found in surah 108 and surah 2. However, I do think that there is a central chiasm at the heart of surah 17 that begins in verse 53 and ends in verse 65. The following is the basic outline of the chiasm.

A – Satan (53)
   B – take charge of them (54)
      C – signs and warning (59)
         D – knowledge of people (60)
      C' – vision and warning (60)
   B' – rouse them (64)
A' – Satan (64)

First, I want to point out that there might be more elements to this chiasm than I have identified here, but for present purposes these components are adequate to support my interpretation. Satan is mentioned in the outer elements of the chiasm (A-A'), and in both cases he is set up as the enemy of humanity, leading people astray and making false promises. In the next pairing (B-B'), a contrast is established between what the Prophet is able to do and what Satan is able to do. In verse 54, the Prophet is told that he was not sent to take charge of humanity, and in verse 64 Satan is charged with trying to distract humanity by whatever means he can. The next component (C-C') establishes that the purpose of signs from God is as a warning for people, and it also serves to link Muhammad with other prophets.

In the first part of verse 60 we read that "your Lord knows all about human beings." This, to my mind, is the key message of the surah, and to some extent a key component of the overall message of the Qur'an. It matches the central element of the "Throne verse" (see chapter 9), and, given its position near the center of the Qur'an, it reinforces the idea that while the Qur'an is a guidance for people, as outlined in surah 1, humanity needs protection from the evil one "who whispers into the hearts of people" (114:5).

Prelude

Glory to Him who made His servant travel by night from the sacred place of worship to the furthest place of worship, whose surroundings We have blessed, to show him some of Our signs: He alone is the All Hearing, the All Seeing. (17:1)

Both thematically and linguistically this verse appears to stand apart from the rest of surah 17. No direct reference to a night journey made by Muhammad is found anywhere else in this surah or in the rest of the Qur'an. At the same time, this verse has given rise to endless theological speculation as well as providing the basis for a vast mystical literature and artistic tradition within Islam (Vuckovic 2004), especially arising out of the elaborated version of the story as presented in the biography of the Prophet by Ibn Ishaq (see chapter 1).

Journeys are an important literary device that is employed in all forms of literature, from scripture, to epics like Homer's *Odyssey*, and on to more recent widely-read works of fiction such as Joseph Conrad's *Heart of Darkness* and Paul Coelho's *The Alchemist*. The vast majority of the text of the Torah is taken up with recounting the wanderings in the wilderness of Moses and the Hebrew people as they travel from Egypt to the Promised Land. Similarly, Filson (1970) demonstrates how this device is skillfully employed by the one of the writers of the New Testament, pointing out that forty percent of the Gospel of Luke is devoted to the journey of Jesus from Galilee to Jerusalem and one-third of the book of Acts is taken up with Paul's journey to Rome. Without digressing into a lengthy discussion on the establishment of the Christian Church, I think it is instructive to observe that while Jesus had Jerusalem as his final destination, thus in some sense signaling continuity with the Jews, Paul shifted the geographic focus of the early Christian community to what was in his lifetime the seat of secular authority (the Roman Empire), and what would become the seat of the Papacy (the Roman Catholic Church).

Borrowing another term from musical analysis, I use the word prelude to describe the function of this verse, basically because it comes before the rest of the surah. However, unlike a prologue, which serves to introduce thematic elements or link verses from one surah to another, a prelude is used to establish a certain tone or expectation by alluding to familiar material, while at the same time introducing something new and different. There are several elements in this verse that require explanation.

The concept of a night journey is nothing new, for as Robinson (2003: 191) observes, there are three places in the Qur'an (20:77, 26:52, 44:23) where the expression is used with reference to the escape from

Pharaoh by Moses and the Hebrews. What is new, and in some way miraculous, is that God causes Muhammad to travel by night from one physical location to another, clearly something impossible for a mere mortal. The astonishing character of this event would not be lost on those hearing this verse, as they would likely associate the two places of worship with Makkah and Jerusalem. From a theological perspective, the declaration that both of these locations are considered blessed serves to link Islam with Judaism, and to link Muhammad with Abraham and the other prophets. The fact that Muhammad is shown various signs again serves to reinforce his legitimacy as a prophet, but it also acts as a reminder that others before Muhammad have received signs from God. The use of the divine names (All Hearing, All Seeing) at the end of the verse is a familiar signal that a transition is about to take place in the text, and the selection of these particular divine names might suggest that even though Muhammad has been chosen to receive the revelation (hear the Qur'an) and has been allowed to see various signs, his hearing and seeing are nothing compared to what God can hear and see.

Even though there are no further direct references to the night journey, the idea of a journey does appear at various other places throughout the surah. In verse 12, the creation of night and day are explained partially as a means for people to measure the passage of time, and thus have an awareness of their journey through life. On a more mystical level, in verse 60, there is a brief mention of the vision shown to Muhammad, but it is not clear that this is reference to the vision mentioned in the first verse, or whether perhaps this refers more generally to the revelation of the Qur'an. In verses 66 through 70, there is a reference to travel by ship in search of God's bounty, introducing a spatial component to the idea of a journey, to go along with the temporal component described in verse 12. Finally, in verse 93, the notion of Muhammad ascending into the sky is mentioned, again introducing a more mystical interpretation to the journey idea, but also highlighting that what is impossible for humans is easy for God.

Concluding Remarks

As I stated at the outset, the purpose of this book was to provide a guidebook for those people who were trying to read the Qur'an in an English translation, and who gave up because they found the text for one reason or another to be too foreign. For a start, I hope that I have been able to demonstrate that there is a structural and thematic integrity to the Qur'an that might not be apparent upon initially reading the text, but that emerges when the text is approached in a systematic and open manner. I have tried to illustrate a way to explore the Qur'an, by suggesting a reading order, providing a number of analytical techniques drawn from literary analysis, and by focusing more on context and thematic content than on linguistic elements. At the same time, my approach, and the material that I have been able to cover in this book, does not provide a comprehensive, definitive, or in any way authoritative treatment of what is contained in the Qur'an. Rather, my reading of the Qur'an reflects my academic and religious background and my experience with the analysis of sacred and secular texts.

Reflecting a couple of the concepts raised in surah 17, reading the Qur'an is very much a journey, and unlike reading the Torah or many other literary works, the path is not so much from beginning to end as it is across and through, as if moving around a matrix or network. I have outlined a potential order in which to begin reading the Qur'an, but once a reader is comfortable with the structure of the Qur'an, it is just as valuable to open the book at any point and start reading. However, as emphasized in surah 17, reading the Qur'an must be done in increments, without haste.

Robert A. Campbell

Bibliography

Abbott, H. 2008. *The Cambridge Introduction to Narrative*, 2nd ed. Cambridge: Cambridge University Press.

Alter, R. 1981. *The Art of Biblical Narrative*. New York: Basic Books.

Armstrong, K. 1991. *Muhammad*. London: Orion House.

Baldick, C. 2001. *The Concise Oxford Dictionary of Literary Terms*. Oxford: Oxford University Press.

Breck, J. 1994. *The Shape of Biblical Language: Chiasmus in the Scriptures and Beyond*. Crestwood, NY: St. Vladimir's Seminary Press.

Brodie, T. L. 2001. *Genesis as Dialogue*. Oxford: Oxford University Press.

Bucaille, M. 1979. *The Bible, the Qur'an and Science*. Indianapolis: American Trust Publications.

Chabbi, J. 2003. Jinn. In *Encyclopedia of the Qur'an*, edited by J. Dammen McAuliffe, Vol. 3, 43-49. Leiden: Brill.

Chittick, W. C. 1989. *The Sufi Path to Knowledge*. Albany, NY: SUNY Press.

Cleary, T. 2001. *The Wisdom of the Prophet*. Boston: Shambhala.

Cook, D. 2002. *Studies in Muslim Apocalyptic*. Princeton: Darwin Press.

Cook, D. 2005. *Contemporary Muslim Apocalyptic Literature*. Syracuse, NY: Syracuse University Press.

Crone, P., and M. Cook. 1977. *Hagarism: The Making of the Islamic World*. Cambridge: Cambridge University Press.

Dakake, M. M. 2004. The Soul as Barzakh: Substantial Motion and Mulla Sadra's Theory of Human Becoming. *Muslim World* 94: 107-30.

Dorsey, D. A. 1999. *The Literary Structure of the Old Testament: A Commentary on Genesis-Malachi*. Grand Rapids: Baker Books.

Esack, F. 2005. *The Qur'an: A User's Guide*. Oxford: Oneworld.

Fahd, T. 2001. Divination. In *Encyclopedia of the Qur'an*, edited by J. Dammen McAuliffe, Vol. 1, 542-45. Leiden: Brill.

Filson, F. V. 1970. The Journey Motif in Luke-Acts. In *Apostolic History and the Gospel*, edited by W. W. Gasque and R. P. Martin, 68-77. Exeter: Paternoster Press.

Freitag, S. B. 2007. South Asian Ways of Seeing, Muslim Ways of Knowing. *Indian Economic & Social History Review* 44: 297-331.

Ghazali, M. al-. 2000. *A Thematic Commentary on the Qur'an*. London: International Institute of Islamic Thought.

Haleem, M. Abdel. 1999. *Understanding the Qur'an*. New York: I.B. Tauris.

Haleem, M. Abdel. 2005. *The Qur'an: A New Translation*. Oxford: Oxford University Press.

Hatley, S. 2007. Mapping the Esoteric Body in the Islamic Yoga of Bengal. *History of Religions* 46: 351-368.

Hawting, G. R. 1999. *The Idea of Idolatry and the Emergence of Islam*. Cambridge: Cambridge University Press.

Iqbal, M. 2004. Abdullah Yusuf Ali & Muhammad Asad: Two Approaches to the English Translation of the Qur'an. In *The Koran: Critical Concepts in Islamic Studies*, edited by C. Turner, Vol. IV, 281-296. New York: Routledge Curzon.

Irwin, R. 2003. *The Arabian Nights: A Companion*. London: Palgrave.

Johns, A. H. 2004. The Quranic Presentation of the Joseph Story: Naturalistic or Formulaic Language? In *The Koran: Critical Concepts in Islamic Studies*, edited by C. Turner, Vol. III, 214-243. New York: Routledge Curzon.

Jomier, J. 2004. The Divine Name "Al-Rahman" in the Qur'an. In *The Koran: Critical Concepts in Islamic Studies*, edited by C. Turner, Vol. II, 345-358. New York: Routledge Curzon.

Kaltner, J. 2003. *Inquiring of Joseph: Getting to Know a Biblical Character through the Qur'an*. Collegeville, MN: Liturgical Press.

Kassis, H. E. 1983. *A Concordance of the Qur'an*. Berkeley: University of California Press.

Khan, I. A. 2005. *Reflections on the Qur'an: Understanding Surahs Al-Fatihah and Al-Baqarah*. Leicestershire, UK: Islamic Foundation.

Kirsch, J. 1998. *Moses: A Life*. New York: Ballantine.

Lings, M. 1983. *Muhammad*. Rochester, VT: Inner Traditions International.

MacDonald, J. 1956. Joseph in the Qur'an and Muslim Commentary: A Comparative Study. *Muslim World* 46: 113-131.

Massey, K. 2003. Mysterious Letters. In *Encyclopedia of the Qur'an*, edited by J. Dammen McAuliffe, Vol. 3, 471-476. Leiden: Brill.

Mir, M. 1986. The Qur'anic Story of Joseph: Plot, Themes, and Characters. *Muslim World* 76: 1-15.

Mir, M. 2004a. Irony in the Qur'an: A Study of the Story of Joseph. In *The Koran: Critical Concepts in Islamic Studies*, edited by C. Turner, Vol. III, 381-394. New York: Routledge Curzon.

Mir, M. 2004b. The Sura as a Unity: A Twentieth Century Development in Qur'an Exegesis. In *The Koran: Critical Concepts in Islamic Studies*, edited by C. Turner, Vol. IV, 198-209. New York: Routledge Curzon.

Morris, J. W. 1994. Dramatizing the Sura of Joseph: An Introduction to the Islamic Humanities. *Journal of Turkish Studies* 18: 201-224.

Mubarakpuri, S. al-. 2002. *The Sealed Nectar*. Riyadh: Darussalam.

Mulla Sadra. 2004. *On the Hermeneutics of the Light Verse of the Qur'an*. Translated, introduced, and annotated by Latimah-Parvin Peerwani. London: ICAS Press.

Murata, S., and W. C. Chittick. 1994. *The Vision of Islam*. St. Paul, MN: Paragon House.

Nasr, S. H. 2006. *Islamic Philosophy from Its Origins to the Present*. Albany, NY: SUNY Press.

Nelson, K. 2001. *The Art of Reciting the Qur'an*. Cairo: The American University in Cairo Press.

Nevo, Y. D., and J. Koren. 2003. *Crossroads to Islam*. Amherst, NY: Prometheus Books.

Omar, A. M. 2003. *Dictionary of the Holy Qur'an*. Rheinfelden, Germany: Noor Foundation.

Ostler, N. 2005. *Empires of the Word*. New York: Harper Collins.

O'Shaughnessy, T. J. 1973. God's Throne and the Biblical Symbolism of the Qur'an. *Numen* 20: 202-221.

Rahman, F. 1994. *Major Themes in the Qur'an*. Minneapolis, MN: Bibliotheca Islamica.

Renard, J. 2001. Alexander. In *Encyclopedia of the Qur'an*, edited by J. Dammen McAuliffe, Vol. 1 61-62. Leiden: Brill.

Rendsburg, G. A. 1988. Literary Structures in the Qur'anic and Biblical Stories of Joseph. *Muslim World* 78: 118-120.

Rippin, A. 2003. Numbers and Enumeration. In *Encyclopedia of the Qur'an*, edited by J. Dammen McAuliffe, Vol. 3, 549-554. Leiden: Brill.

Robinson, N. 2003. *Discovering the Qur'an*, 2nd edition. Washington: Georgetown University Press.

Rodinson, M. 1980. *Muhammad*. New York: New Press.

Saeed, A. 2006. *Interpreting the Qur'an: Towards a Contemporary Approach*. London: Routledge.

Schimmel, A. 1993. *The Mystery of Numbers*. Oxford: Oxford University Press.

Sells, M. 1999. *Approaching the Qur'an: The Early Revelations*. Ashland, OR: White Cloud Press.

Shahid, I. 2004. *Fawatih al-Suwar*: The Mysterious Letters of the Qur'an. In *The Koran: Critical Concepts in Islamic Studies,* edited by C. Turner, Vol. III, 417-431. New York: Routledge Curzon.

Sicker, M. 2000. *The Pre-Islamic Middle East*. Westport, CT: Praeger.

Stern, M. S. 1985. Muhammad and Joseph: A Study of Koranic Narrative. *Journal of Near Eastern Studies* 44: 193-204.

Stoneman, R. 2008. *Alexander the Great: A Life in Legend*. New Haven, CT: Yale University Press.

Stowasser, B. F. 1994. *Women in the Qur'an Traditions, and Interpretation*. Oxford: Oxford University Press.

Varisco, D. M. 2003. Numerology. In *Encyclopedia of the Qur'an,* edited by J. Dammen McAuliffe, Vol. 3, 554-555. Leiden: Brill.

Vuckovic, B. 2004. *Heavenly Journeys, Earthly Concerns: The Legacy of the Mir'aj in the Formation of Islam*. London: Routledge.

Wansbrough, J. 1977. *Quranic Studies: Sources and Methods of Scriptural Interpretation*. Oxford: Oxford University Press.

Welch, J. W. 1981. *Chiasmus in Antiquity: Structures, Analyses, Exegesis*. Hildesheim: Gerstenberg.

Yusuf Ali, A. 2004. *The Meaning of the Holy Qur'an*, 11th ed. Beltsville, MD: Amana Publications.